Children, Power and Schooling

How childhood is structured in the primary school

Dympna Devine

Trentham Books

Stoke on Trent, UK and Sterling, USA

Trentham Books Limited

Westview House	22883 Quicksilver Drive
734 London Road	Sterling
Oakhill	VA 20166-2012
Stoke on Trent	USA
Staffordshire	
England ST4 5NP	

© 2003 Dympna Devine

First published 2003

British Library Cataloguing-in-Publication Data
A catalogue record for this book is available from the British Library

ISBN 1 85856 271 6

Designed and typeset by Trentham Print Design Ltd., Chester and printed in Great Britain by Cromwell Press Ltd., Wiltshire.

Acknowledgements

In the course of working on the research for this book, I have become indebted to a number of people. I would firstly like to thank the children and teachers who participated in this study. Their tolerance of my intrusion into their school lives was greatly appreciated, as was their openness and frankness in working with them. I hope I have done justice to their views and experiences.

I have received much encouragement and support from Sheelagh Drudy, my other colleagues in the Education Department UCD, on the ESAI executive and elsewhere. A special word of thanks to Kathleen Lynch for kindling and encouraging my interest in this area and to Anne Lodge, Máire Nic Ghiolla Phádraig and Jim Deegan for continuing the debates and extending my understanding. Particular thanks also to Jens Qvortrup and Len Barton for their interest and support. To Gillian Klein at Trentham Books for her patience, meticulous work and constructive criticism.

To my family for all their love and support. A special thanks to my parents, and to my sisters – each in their own way a source of inspiration. To Ger, my best friend, and our three boys (Patrick, Cian and Oisín) who bring such joy. To Winnie for looking after us all so well. To my friends for all their care, encouragement and fun.

Finally I would like to thank the editors of the following journals for permission to republish some of the material in this book: *Childhood; International Studies in Sociology of Education; Irish Educational Studies.*

Children, Power and Schooling

How childhood is structured in the primary school

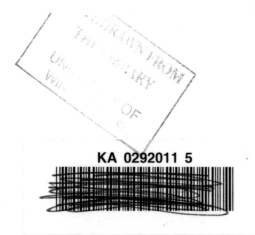

Contents

1
Introduction

Schools are constructed, administered and shaped by adults for children. As social institutions they play a central role in the construction of children's perception of themselves, of the social world and of their place within it. This 'structuring of childhood' through an extended compulsory period of schooling is a relatively recent phenomenon yet appears to be taken for granted as a natural part of childhood in the Western world. Taken for granted especially by adults, who generally attest to the benefits of long term schooling for personal and social development, as well as to economic gain by societies who invest heavily in the education of their young. This book however is written from the perspective of children themselves. It seeks to ascertain their voice on the experience of school. It paints a picture of the schooling experience for a sample of Irish primary school children, raising questions such as: What do these children think of school? Why do they think they go to school? What do they like and dislike about school? How would they change school?

The answers that children provide to these questions indicate not only their attitudes toward school itself but also to the values, dispositions and discourses they draw on in arriving at such evaluations. Given that schools are established, administered and run by adults, yet attended by children, *what* children think about school and *how* they experience being schooled is tied fundamentally to the exercise of power between adults and children. Broader questions

1

related to the experience of this power relation between adults and children are an important aspect of the experience of school and raise issues related to the active participation by children in the organisation of their school lives. We must ask: Do children have a say in school? Who decides what children do in school? Are children treated fairly in school?

How power is exercised between adults and children in school also influences the way children view themselves as children, in particular their perception of themselves as persons with a right to exercise their voice on matters which directly affect them and have their views taken seriously and treated with respect.

Studying childhood and schooling

The idea that children should be treated seriously as persons in their own right, with a voice both to express and to be heard, is relatively new and is given legitimacy in the United Nations Convention on the Rights of the Child (1989). Traditional accounts of children and childhood inspired specifically by developmental psychology have tended to emphasise childhood as a period of 'becoming': the 'irrational' and 'immature' child moves gradually to a rational adult end state. From this viewpoint, childhood is defined as a period of growth and transition through a series of pre-defined stages, each marked by its own essential features and characteristics. Traditional theories of socialisation have reinforced such viewpoints, portraying children primarily as passive recipients of the dominant culture.

Such limited conceptions of childhood have however been critiqued, provoking new modes of thinking and research in the fields of sociology and psychology. Social constructivists articulate a view of human development as dynamic and social, derived from the inter-action of individuals, including children, with their surrounding environment. These emphasise the complexity of children's response to their world and the importance of the cultural and social context in framing children's perceptions and capacities (Benson, 2001; Bruner, 1996; Cooley, 1902; Harré, 1993; Mead, 1972; Vygotsky, 1978 and 1991). Such views challenge an overly passive view of children and emphasise the dynamic reflective interplay between children and their social environment. Research into child culture, for example, demonstrates how children actively explore their emerging identities and capacities with one another (be it in terms of gender, ethnicity, social class, dis/ability), as they sort and select from the myriad of discourses available within their culture (Connolly, 1998; Davies, 1982 and 1991, Devine and Kenny, 2002; James, Jencks and Prout, 1998; Lodge and Flynn, 2001; Sluckin, 1981; Troyna and Hatcher, 1992).

Focusing on the lifeworld of children through the lens of child culture highlights not only important dimensions of children's agency but also the validity of considering children as persons with their own perspectives and ways of viewing the world. A consideration of child culture indicates the limitations of considering children as relatively passive beings and their capacity for actively constructing their own social worlds, free from the constraints and influence of adults.

New ways of thinking about childhood itself have also emerged in recent years. Such thinking, inspired in particular by the sociological study of childhood, emphasises the socially constructed nature of childhood and how this can vary both culturally and historically. Differences in the experience of childhood are evident both between and within generations, differences located in the context of broader cultural, social and economic change (Butler and Shaw, 1996; Cleary *et al*, 2001; James, Jencks and Prout, 1998; Hendrick, 1997; Mayall, 2002; Qvortrup, 1994). Socio-historical analyses of childhood (e.g Ferriter, 2002; Hendrick, 1997; Postman, 1994; Zelizer, 1985) point to the changing conceptions of childhood through the ages and the implications for both the experience of childhood and the ways in which children think/thought about themselves both as children and as persons with particular social, gendered, ethnic identities. The move from rural based economies to urbanised industrialised societies in the last century is a case in point, giving rise to mass state schooling for children. This dramatically changed the manner in which children's time and space, hence childhood, was experienced. Thus the advent of compulsory schooling was a key component in the structuring of modern childhood, regulating, controlling and defining children's lives in a systematic society wide manner.

A further element deriving from such analyses relates to the positioning of children relative to adults in all societies. In particular, childhood is defined as a structural category that carries with it attributes and modes of being by virtue of membership of that category1, which differ from those of the dominant adult group. Issues related to the rights and status of children are brought to the fore and questions are raised as to the manner in which power is exercised between adults and children (Corsaro, 1997; James *et al*, 1998; Mayall, 2002; Qvortrup, 1987 and 1994). Children are deemed to have minority status within society. They are discriminated against on the grounds of their 'immaturity' and perceived 'irrationality'. This book questions traditional paternalistic assumptions regarding child/adult relations and highlights the adult centred focus of much public policy decision making in society (Archard, 1993; Qvortrup, 1987 and 1994), including that which applies to schools.

Sociological analyses of schools have traditionally exhibited this paternalistic trend, focusing on the reproductive role of schooling and the importance of education for the socialisation of the young into the culture and value system of the adult world. In the functionalist analyses of Durkheim (1956) and Parsons (1951) for example, the child is portrayed as dependent on the adult population (parents, teachers, those in authority) to guide, direct and feed her/his needs in such a way as to ensure successful integration into adult society. In Marxist analyses, schooling is perceived as an important tool used by the bourgeoisie to ensure hegemonic dominance and studies of school focus on the communication of beliefs, practices etc. that serve to reproduce inequalities based on gender, social class and ethnicity that exist in the broader society (e.g. Apple, 1986; Bourdieu, 1977 and 1993; Bowles and Gintis, 1976; Lynch, 1989). Many of these latter studies focus on schools at a systems level, underplaying the lived reality of the day to day experience of schooling.

Qualitative research in the sociology of education documents life in schools and classrooms and paints a more dynamic picture of schooling that construes children as active contributors to school life and culture, rather than as passive recipients. A wealth of such research has been conducted in the past twenty years (e.g. Connolly, 1998; Lodge and Flynn, 2001; Lynch and Lodge, 2002; Montandon and Osiek, 1998; Pollard, 1985 and 1996; Pollard and Triggs, 2000; Troyna and Hatcher, 1992; Woods, 1990) that supports and co-incides with developments in the broader sociology of childhood. However, the direct issue of how schooling structures childhood, in particular arising from the manner in which power is exercised be-tween adults and children, has not been adequately explored. Further, while power has been identified frequently as a salient feature of school life (e.g Bernstein, 1975; Jackson, 1968) and is implied in much of the sociological analyses of schooling, children's perspective on the exercise of power in school has received little attention. This book seeks to fill this gap and identify, represent and analyse children's views of school.

As policy makers increasingly try to take on board these new ways of thinking about children and childhood (e.g. the National Children's Strategy 2000 in Ireland) the importance of considering children's experience and perspectives on schooling is opportune. Recommendations regarding greater sensitivity to children's rights, for example, can only be properly made when informed by the views and perspectives of children themselves. With respect to schooling, this book is an important step in that process.

Research design and methodology

Research was conducted with a sample of primary school children in the Republic of Ireland over one school year. In total 133 children from three primary schools were selected, ranging in age from 7 to 11 years. While each school was co-educational, they differed in terms of social class intake, with Table 1 on page 6 indicating the precise classification of each of the schools in the sample.

Parkway is located in a working class estate characterised by a high unemployment rate and predominantly public housing. Hillview is located in a private housing estate and employment patterns are mainly in the trade and service sectors. Churchfield is located in a very affluent area with pockets of social disadvantage and employ-ment patterns are generally in the professional and managerial sectors.

Table 1: Sample for the study

School	Social Classification	Number of pupils in the study	Number of classes	Grade Level
Parkway	Working Class	49	2	1, 2 and 5
Hillview	Lower Mid. Class	25	1	5
Churchfield	Middle Class	59	2	2 and 5
Totals		133	5	

While the consent of all children involved in the research was obtained directly from the children themselves (as well as their parents), reassurances were constantly sought and given as to the confidentiality of the children's views, especially in light of any negative comments they would make about their school experience (reflecting my sensitivity to the power dimension in pupil/teacher relations). Although the focus of the research lay predominantly in ascertaining children's views and experiences, semi-structured interviews were also conducted with classroom teachers and school principals. Since the research was conducted over a period of one school year there were many opportunities for informal conversations with teaching and support staff in all three schools.

The research employed a mixed methodology that included the use of extended observations of class and schoolyard activity, sociometric analysis, semi-structured interviews, questionnaires, diary records kept by the children themselves and children's drawings. Interviews with children were predominantly carried out in friendship groups of three to four, although occasionally children asked to be interviewed on their own, especially if they were unsure of their friendship allegiances. Over the course of the school year, I became familiar to the children and teachers alike, making my presence less conspicuous as the year went by and building a relationship of trust with those directly involved in the study. Teachers gradually relaxed in their classrooms in spite of the intrusion of another adult taking copious notes at the back of the classroom. My insistence that I would sit in a child's chair, in spite of initial efforts by teachers to provide more comfortable seating for me was important in showing the children that I was not to be regarded in the same light as other adults in the school. Similarly my tendency to ignore/not report children's misdemeanors was important in building up the trust that was to be established over the course of the school year.[2]

Gaining access to the classrooms is only the first step; I also needed to establish the teachers' trust. I continually reassured the teachers that what I was observing was the processes taking place in the classroom and not the quality of work teachers were engaged in. In my relations with both teachers and pupils I had to negotiate a fine balance in terms of time spent getting to know each group. Detailed field notes were taken at each stage of observation and both teachers and pupils were given access to these if they so wished. Although I usually spent breaks in the playground with the children, I occasionally went instead to the staffroom. Listening to staffroom talk about the children was an important part of the research process. It enabled me to build a fuller picture of the views, motivations, anxieties, tensions and joys of teaching.

How this book is organised

The book is arranged in eight chapters. While the main focus is upon the children's perspectives, the analysis is interspersed with the views and perspectives of teachers. A number of key questions run through the analysis:

How do the children experience schooling?

What does the children's perspective tell us about the exercise of power between adults and children and the structuring of childhood through school?

In what ways do children exercise agency in school and how does this influence the exercise of power between adults and children?

Chapters 2–6 present perspectives on the experience of schooling. For the purposes of analysis, this is divided into four main categories: social relations, curriculum, pedagogy and evaluation. Chapter 2 outlines the children's perspectives on their social relations in school, especially their relations with teachers and peers. The dynamics of power and control in teacher/pupil relations emerge strongly in the analysis. The importance of children's own world of child culture is also brought to light, as their friendships with peers helps them cope with the demands of classroom life. Chapter 3 documents the children's views on what they learn, presenting their likes and dislikes as well as the subject areas they consider to be most important in school. Key values implicit in the children's assumptions about the curriculum are considered, particularly as this relates to the exercise of power and the structuring of childhood.

The area of pedagogy is explored over two chapters. Chapter 4 outlines the overall pedagogical context by detailing teachers' perspectives and views as well as observational data related to teacher practice in each of the classrooms. Chapter 5 presents the children's perspectives as this relates to the control of their time and space in school. Issues related to school rules and discipline as well as teaching practices are examined. The experience of being evaluated is the subject of Chapter 6, in which the children's views on both formal and informal evaluation procedures are explored.

The findings outlined in Chapters 2 – 6 provide the context for the broad based theoretical analysis of child/adult relations presented in Chapter 7. This analysis is informed by the work of Foucault on the exercise of power in modern societies and Giddens on the structuration of social systems. I explore the tension between structure and agency, two central tenets in social theory, as this applies to our understanding of childhood. A model identifying the cyclical interwoven nature of the exercise of power in modern institutions such as schools is developed, drawing on the voices and experiences of children as recounted here. This model forms the basis for considering the policy implications of the study and these are outlined in Chapter 8.

Notes

1 Such analyses coincides with the use of age generally as a marker of social identity, in the same way as gender, social class, ethnicity etc. have traditionally been used in sociological analysis to classify and group the population in social terms.

2 A particular incident in Hillview illustrates this sharply. It was the third day of my observation and the class teacher had left the classroom, opening the door of an adjacent classroom to inform the teacher there to 'keep an eye' on her class while she went to the office. The children were engaged in artwork and a group began to sing aloud. They kept glancing in my direction to see if I was going to reprimand or stop them. But I just kept writing notes in my field diary without comment. The supervising teachers entered the room and reprimanded the children for singing. Each child in turn denied that they were responsible for 'starting it'. When the class teacher returned, a 'major' investigation was begun as to who was responsible for all the noise. The teachers resisted the temptation to seek clarification from me and the children en masse were reprimanded. The incident was highly significant in highlighting my non-authoritarian role as researcher to both the children and the teachers. It also reassured children that their 'back-stage' behaviour would not to be reported by the researcher, thus facilitating the gathering of data related to this important aspect of school experience.

2

How Pupils View Social Relations in School

Introduction

The school environment is a highly social one in which both teachers' and pupils' identities are simultaneously challenged and affirmed. Utilising the concepts of coping strategies and frame, Pollard's work in particular (1985, 1990, 1996, 2000) demonstrates how teachers and pupils struggle and negotiate with one another, striving to maintain a positive sense of self in their school lives. However, the conduct of pupil/teacher relations does not occur in a vacuum and is intimately connected to the exercise of power between adults and children in school. Through their relations with their teachers children form perspectives on what is valued and important in their education, as well as how they themselves as children are valued and respected within the school. Teachers for their part draw on a range of adult discourses related to education, schooling and childhood in their classroom practice, framing their relations with their pupils in terms of adult defined goals and expectations. Power is exercised in this process of interaction and reaction, as teachers control the time and space of children in school.

From the children's perspective, their relations with adults is but one, albeit significant, aspect of their social experience in school. Children's relations with their peers and their participation in a world of childhood games and rituals (child culture) frame much of their attitude toward and experience of school. Research conducted into this aspect of school life highlights children's capacity for creativity and agency as they relate to one another in terms of rules and regulations that are clearly defined and understood in their social world (Blatchford, 1989 and 1996; Connolly, 1998; Davies, 1991; Opie and Opie, 1991; Sluckin, 1981; Woods, 1990). In this process children exercise power with one another, positioning themselves in relation to one another in terms of their status and popularity, the latter influenced by factors such as age, gender, ethnicity etc.

This chapter considers these issues. It breaks the analysis into two distinct areas: patterns of pupil/teacher relations and the exercise of power and patterns of peer relations and the exercise of power. Conclusions are drawn with reference to the implications of social relations for the structuring of childhood in school.

Perspectives on pupil/teacher relations and the exercise of power

The analysis begins by highlighting perceptions of power and control between teachers and pupils with particular reference to the difference in status between the groups. Two areas in which such differences are prominent relate to children's perception of being treated fairly and the extent to which they feel they can exercise a voice in school. Positive aspects of pupil/teacher relations are highlighted with teacher interviews and observational data included where appropriate.

Perceptions of power and control in the pupil/teacher relationship

In their discussion of the power exercised by teachers in school, it was clear that children perceived such power to be manifest in two distinct yet interrelated areas. The first concerned status and the exercise of authority, while the second related to freedom of expression and the lack of reciprocity in pupil/teacher relations in school. In their accounts of difference in status between themselves and their teachers, children expressed a keen awareness of status hierarchies in the school, with themselves positioned at the bottom of this hierarchy:

> Mr _____ (Principal) is the most important cos he runs the school, then Mr _____ (Vice principal), the teachers and the children are the last... we are important to our mams... you don't see the children out doing big money deals or bossing others... children don't boss adults (Grade 5 boy, Hillview)

> The children are the least important cos we are just children (Grade 5 girl, Hillview)

Such status derived from being an adult and grown up and bestowed on teachers the power to 'boss' and control children, and generally tell them what to do:

> The children have the least power cos they're not allowed do anything... say what they want, do what they want... the principal has the most power and the teachers... they're grown up so they're meant to be the bosses (Grade 5 boy, Parkway)

Interestingly, however, some children did express the view that they were the most important in the school, not because they were children, but because they provided work for teachers and were the basis for the existence of the school in the first place:

> I'd say the pupils are the most important cos we're their job... .you have to have pupils to teach... we are giving them work to do cos they want work and we are giving it to them (Grade 5 boy, Hillview)

> we are important to the school cos if there were no children there would be no school... we're actually more important than the principal cos if we weren't here he would have no work (Grade 5 boy, Hillview)

Being treated with respect is an important indicator of status and just over half the children in the study agreed with the statement that they were treated with respect in school. Age appeared to be an important factor here with older children more likely to criticise the amount of respect shown by teachers toward them in school[1]. This perceived absence of respect was reflected in the amount of work older children were required to do as well as the level of control exercised over them on a daily basis:

> your made feel important when you are treated with respect... like we treat them with respect... we practically lick the dirt off

their feet and what do we get back?... work... we are supposed
to get work I know but not that much... (Grade 5 boy, Hillview)

No way are the children respected... let us have more... we
should have a say in making rules for them, making rules for
us, and our clothes... I hate this uniform (Grade 5 girl, Hillview)

The second aspect of the children's concern over teacher power
related to the greater freedom of expression afforded teachers in
their relations with pupils and correspondingly the absence of
reciprocity (an important value within child culture) in pupil interactions with their teachers. Thus older children commented on the
freedom of teachers to display their mood and the inability of children, by virtue of their child status, to respond in kind:

shouting at us she nearly bursts me eardrums... and she's
moaning that she's getting a headache over us shouting?... but
if we say: 'ah miss will you be quiet and just talk normal' 'oh
don't you tell me what to do, get up to the principal's office'...
and we'd be suspended (Grade 5 boy, Parkway)

in the classroom the teachers and the principal have the most
power cos we can't give out to them like they do to us... we
can't tell them to shut up or go up to the office... they are adults
and they think they have more power... but kids have rights as
well (Grade 5 boy, Hillview)

This awareness of a lack of reciprocity is also evident in the children's comments that they would like to see greater empathy on the
part of teachers over what it is like to be a child, drawing comparisons in this respect between their home and school experiences:

at home they care about you more... and you have more freedom... there's fewer children at home... and you don't have to
be working all the time... that's the thing about school... it's
nearly all work and you get tired... (Grade 5 boy, Churchfield)

they are always on at you... don't be slouching in the chair... sit
up straight... your mam and dad don't say that... they know
that's the way you want to be comfortable (Grade 5 girl , Hillview)[2]

In typifying teachers in terms of the power they hold, it is clear that
children perceive themselves in opposite terms – as holding little

power in school in their relations with teachers. Interviews with teachers suggest a different picture, however. All teachers in the study expressed the view that children today were more forward, outgoing and mature than they had been in the past and were quick to assert their rights in their interactions with adults:

> Children today are much more independent... they are given much more confidence, they're more knowledgeable about their rights, much more demanding... they know what they should have and they expect you to produce the results... so you have pressure from them not just the parents expecting results (Grade 2 teacher, Churchfield)

> they're much more forward and know more about their rights... they hear about it at home, they know what they are entitled to (Grade 5 teacher, Hillview)

All agreed that adults interacted differently today with children than in the past and this was perceived to be generally a good thing. Such change was reflected in the abolition of corporal punishment and in the more open and sensitive approach by teachers in their interaction with children:

> when we were kids in school there was a lot of picking on the soft kids and it wasn't seen to be a problem... it must have been terrible for children in the past... absolutely hell for children with low self-esteem... it's a positive thing for children today... the greater sensitivity to them and the elimination of corporal punishment (Principal, Parkway)

> I think children appear more confident because we interact differently with them than the teachers we had... you didn't get an opportunity to express your opinion in class, to talk in class... you listened and did what you were told and that's it (Grade 2 teacher, Hillview)

The teachers' comments suggest that they are aware of changes in the discourses and norms governing child/adult interactions. Such changes are welcomed, but only in so far as the teacher role is not questioned and where teacher authority is unquestioned. Thus, teachers speak of the benefits of being more caring and sensitive in dealing with children, but the assertion of children's rights and the tendency to question and challenge teachers is met with some scepticism. This undoubtedly relates to concerns among teachers regarding the maintenance of control in their classrooms and identified by other researchers in the field (e.g. King, 1978 and 1989; Osborn *et al*, 2000; O'Sullivan, 1980; Pollard, 1985; Spencer, 2000; Watkinson, 1996).

The data suggests then that the exercise of power and the maintenance of control are central elements in the dynamic interplay between teachers and their students in school. Children clearly view differences between themselves and their teachers in terms of such control, the older children being particularly sensitive and critical of the differences in power between themselves and their teachers. In four of the five classrooms observed, teacher control was relatively complete, with teachers using their authoritative position to full effect and children responding to teacher instructions and requests with a minimum of fuss. Grade 5 in Parkway however, provides a telling contrast, with the teacher constantly having to 'battle' over the children's voices (mostly boys) and struggle to have herself heard. Boys in this classroom, like the lads in Willis' classic study (1977), demonstrated their indifference to teacher authority by constantly testing her and challenging the boundaries of pupil/ teacher interaction. A tentative control was maintained, dependent primarily on using rewards and tolerating more pupil misdemeanours than I saw allowed in the other classrooms in the study. Pupil responses in this classroom were totally unlike the relative acquiescence to teacher authority evident in all the other classrooms observed. Such differences may be explained in part by the different social class backgrounds of pupils in each school. Children in Hillview and Churchfield (middle class schools) were more confident about the longterm benefits of attention to learning in school (Bourdieu and Passeron, 1977). However, such acquiescence should not necessarily be construed as total acceptance of the teacher role, as I will show.

Perceptions of being treated fairly in school

Children's perception of the differences in status between themselves and teachers rests on the fairness with which they feel they are treated in school. When asked if they had ever been treated unfairly, over half the children in the study (54%) said they had, while 34%

stated they had not. The children's views were influenced by age level and gender, with older girls more likely to state that they had been unfairly treated in school. When asked to specify in what way they had been treated unfairly, the children identified reasons related predominantly to adult power and control (e.g. not being listened to by the teacher (21%), being unfairly punished (36%) and being ignored by the teacher (8%)), while being teased, an aspect of child culture, was mentioned by 34% of these children.

In interviews the children highlighted their annoyance over unfair treatment and some linked it to the subordinate status of children and their inability to assert themselves in the face of adult power:

> when adults are treated unfairly they stand up and object to it... but they don't kinda take children seriously... they just think they are messing or looking for attention (Grade 5 girl, Church-field)

> It's just that say the principal gives you a two page essay for something you didn't do and you say I didn't do that and some teachers think you are being cheeky... but you are just telling the truth... that's what I mean by listening to the child... they don't often listen (Grade 5 boy, Hillview)

Children gave other examples of unfair treatment, such as the breaking of promises and that some teachers had 'pets'. Being the teacher's pet meant receiving favoured treatment and being picked to do favoured activities:

> Mary has a real advantage cos on her birthday for example... we are not usually allowed wear track suits and all her friends were allowed cos they were going to her house after for a party... whereas if we asked it would be a definite no... just because she's the principal's daughter (Grade 5 girl, Church-field)

> the teacher gives most attention to Patricia, and Ann and George... they are all sent on jobs (Grade 5 girls, Hillview)

Favouritism emerged as a particularly contentious issue between boys and girls, with each gender perceiving that the other received the most attention from the teacher. Boys complained mainly because they felt they were reprimanded more than girls. Girls perceived unfairness as centred around being invisible to the teacher, so that they received less attention than the boys:

> our teacher is always picking the boys for something... if they have their hand up she ignores the girls (Grade 5 girls, Parkway)

> if the girls have a fight the teachers just say: 'oh well shake hands and make up' but the boys get extra homework or suspended (Grade 5 boy, Churchfield)

Observational data confirms these children's comments, with boys repeatedly reprimanded to a greater extent than girls (even when girls were guilty of wrong doing). The relative invisibility of girls in the classroom was especially notable in grade 5 in Parkway, best exemplified in the centring of Physical Education around the interests of the boys. Football was played in every PE lesson and the teacher acknowledged that 'to be honest the girls are a bit neglected'. Lessons often began with the teacher declaring: 'Right boys!' as if there were no girls present. The girls in this class remained relatively silent throughout the day. They spoke to the teacher when spoken to but did not actively participate in many of the lessons. This pattern was not as evident in either Hillview or Churchfield. However the inattentive behaviour of most girls in the study tended to take the form of solitary activities such as colouring, that did not threaten the overall learning environment of the classrooms. As a result, they were only occasionally reprimanded and this matches other research in the field. This matches other research in the field (e.g. Drudy and Ui Chatháin, 1999; Paetcher, 1998). Interviews with teachers indicated that in general they perceived girls to be a more homogeneous group who typically tended to please, work well and stay out of trouble. Conversely, boys were perceived to be more challenging and dominant in the classroom:

> The girls tend to achieve much better because the expectation is that they can write neatly, sit down in their place and draw nice pictures whereas the boys aren't into that. It doesn't mean the girls are any brighter it's just what's expected... in concentration level boys would be a lot more giddy, demand more of your attention and the girls are much more willing to please... in general the girls are better behaved (Grade 2 teacher, Churchfield)

> The girls are more reliable and far more independent than the boys... give them anything and they will get on with it. Take misbehaviour... who do you see standing outside of the office more often? ... boys (Grade 5 teacher, Hillview)

When teachers gave boys special attention, it was not always appreciated by the boys themselves, as it challenged their emerging masculinities as tough and independent (see e.g. Connolly, 1998; Mac an Ghaill, 1999). The following comments in Parkway highlight this:

> She cares for us... for our work... a bit too much... she's too protective... she really looks after you... but when your a man you can look after yourself... she wants us to do well... too much (Grade 5 boy, Parkway)

> She should be giving us all work but she shouldn't be giving out to us... but she's always giving out to me cos she's licking up to me as well and I don't like that... I'd rather her be giving out to me... cos she's licking up to me so I won't lose me temper... it's better than getting licked up to... she hates me so she only licks up to me so I won't get mad and I hate that (Grade 5 boy, Parkway)

Exercising a voice in school

The views expressed by the children suggest that their perception of being treated unfairly by teachers centres on not having or being given a voice in what happens in school. The direct questioning of children in terms of whether or not they should have a say in school is interesting in revealing the dominant discourses in children's own minds relating to their rights and status in school. Just under half the sample of children said that children should have a say in school, while a further 33% stated that children should have a say sometimes. When the children were asked to specify the reasons for their responses they were classified as follows (see Table 2.1).

The children's responses were significantly related to both their age level and their social class, with younger children, especially those from Parkway, most likely to insist they were not old enough to have a say, while middle class children, especially those who were older most likely to stress that children have the right to exercise a voice

Table 2.1 Reasons why children should|should not have a say in school

Reasons why children should have a say:	N	%
I would feel listened to	30	22.6
Exercise a greater choice	24	18.0
Children's rights	26	19.5
Reasons why children should not have a say:		
Children are not old enough	19	14.3
Children would be punished	1	0.8
No Answer	33	24.8
Totals	133	100.0

in school. The following comments made during interviews are indicative of the different views expressed:

> We're too young to be in charge... we're smaller than the big people (Grade 2, boy, Churchfield)

> The children should be allowed make the rules sometimes... well not make them but have their say in it... have their opinion... it could be organised at assembly... I suppose the teachers think the children would have lots of fights and things and they would be bold[3] (Grade 5 girl, Hillview)

> I think the children should get a say in deciding the rules... well there are votes for Presidents or whatever so we could put our vote in the box... she'd have her rules and then we'd vote for them (Grade 5 girl, Churchfield)

The diversity in viewpoints expressed by the children is also reflected in the views and opinions of teachers. Differences were identified between teachers in the degree to which they felt children should be consulted or involved in decisions in school. Most teachers cited large class size, time constraints, the perceived immaturity of children and the learning of self-control as reasons for the absence of any consultation with children over what happened in school:

> I don't see there is a place for the children to be telling or ruling the school at this stage... I think where will it ever end this thing of giving them their say and they also have to learn how to make the right decision and be given examples of the right decision... they should participate in decisions as a privilege rather than of right... and if it suits the running of the school (Grade 2 teacher, Churchfield)

> At this age there should be little consultation... I don't think they are mature enough... I mean if they had their way they'd be out playing games twenty four hours a day and they wouldn't see the importance of academic achievement and mucking under doing maths and Irish or whatever... so these are decisions you have to make for them (Principal, Parkway)

Encapsulated in such comments is a discourse on children which perceives them as being incapable of acting responsibly and as in need of containment. A minority, however, appeared to be more open to the concept and were critical of the lack of decision making in school structures:

> I think of lunchtime... we decide what they eat, when they eat, how they eat... they don't even have a choice in that... and I think that's poor especially for the bigger children. The younger children still need to be guided on what's good for them but the older children are well able to understand things but they are never given any decision making in what's important for them now some of them are mature enough... take homework as an example... I know children don't want to do it but what I'm saying is that they should be given an input into what their homework is... not whether they do it or not... it's important for them that we listen to them... they should at least be consulted (Grade 5 teacher, Hillview)

> I think children should have a certain amount of involvement... maybe 50/50... ideally they should have a good part in decisions but sometimes our system doesn't allow this... the rules were set down years ago by adults and now it would be very hard to change them... the curriculum is supposed to be child centred in theory but in practice I wouldn't call it child-centred (Grade 5 teacher, Parkway)

Involving children in decisions is closely linked to listening to them, yet when I asked about possibly establishing structures to give children a greater voice in school I was met with relative silence. It was as if such a concept was outside of the teachers' consciousness and not part of their understanding of what teaching was about, a finding identified in other research in the field (Brennan, 2000). Indeed one teacher in Hillview commented that children were only listened to at a subconscious level when their body language indicated boredom or indifference to a particular lesson:

> I think we listen without consciously thinking we are listening...
> like you start off on a Monday morning with an Irish lesson and
> you think. 'Ah they're asleep we'll move on to something
> else'... they're showing passively they're not ready for this and
> so you go on, in that kind of way, subconsciously even (Grade
> 5 teacher Hillview)

Interestingly, the principals in both Parkway and Churchfield recounted incidences where children (none of whom were in the present study) actively resisted following a decision which had been
made for them. In Parkway, children refused to leave the hall in
protest that the teacher had not used all the PE time available and in
Churchfield, children protested with placards in the yard when it was
decided that they would wear their uniforms during an out of school
religious ceremony. In each instance, the principals came down
firmly on the children: 'they were told to get back to their classrooms and start working or else' (Principal Parkway), in the belief
that their priority in such situations was not to undermine the
authority and position of the teachers:

> Maybe the children had a point... their PE was cut short and
> they love it so much... you see teachers aren't always right and
> that's something you can lose sight of... but I have to protect
> the teachers at all times and I always do and sometimes
> parents come in here complaining to me about so and so and
> I know in my heart and soul they are right but I cannot say
> that... and that is a big problem for me... I have to defend the
> defenceless sometimes and that isn't fair either (Principal,
> Parkway)

> I would generally be willing to try and change for example yard
> times to make more space for the children but there isn't the
> willingness of the staff to do so... where a decision has to be
> made it has to be made and probably not to the favour of the
> children (Principal, Churchfield)

Their comments reveal the position of children within the school
hierarchy: in both instances the interests of teachers as a group take
precedence over those of the children when their interests clashed.

The data suggests competing perceptions of what it is to be a child,
particularly a child in school, with corresponding implications for
definitions of the teacher role. Where children express dissatis-

faction with how they are treated in school (either in specific incidences they described as unfair or because they were not given the
opportunity to voice their opinions) their dissatisfaction arises from
a desire to be taken seriously by adults and be treated with respect
by them. This view, which questions the traditional authority of
teachers, was most often expressed by older children, in particular
those of a middle class background. For the most part, teachers
appear to treat such discourse with suspicion and disregard, relying
on a paternalistic framework to justify the absence of genuine consultation with children over their experience in school.

Positive indicators of pupil/teacher interaction

It would be a mistake, however, to interpret the exercise of power by
teachers in their social interaction with children in wholly negative
terms. Teachers also wield considerable influence over children in
terms of their capacity to praise and reward them for their efforts in
school. All children, especially the youngest, are sensitive to this
form of adult control. It was evident in this study from the fact that
of the 76% of those who stated that there were things which made
them feel good about themselves at school, over half indicated issues
that directly related to teacher influence such as: praise, being good,
finishing their work and doing their work correctly.

Children's priorities in their relations with teachers were evident from
the manner in which they talked about their teachers, with a majority
emphasising in their talk how the teacher interacted with them (by
being patient/impatient, kind/cross, polite, moody/good humoured)
as well as their teaching skills (e.g. how good they were at explaining
things). Some differences between age levels were notable. Younger
children for example were more likely to highlight the affective and
personal dimension of their interactions with teachers:

> she is quite tall and slim, most of the time she is kind, she will
> be married next year (Grade 2 boy, Churchfield)

> a good teacher is someone who likes you, who cares for you
> and who minds you if you fall (Grade 2 girl, Churchfield)

While older children also mentioned positive aspects to their relations with teachers, this was counterbalanced by a tendency to also
highlight issues related to discipline and the exercise of power:

> She's very nice and she doesn't give out a lot. She's never up-tight and she listens when you have something to say. Also she's very clever (Grade 5 boy, Churchfield)

> My teacher is kind to people that are kind to her. It is just like you scratch my back and I'll scratch yours. She is bad to people that are bad to her (Grade 5 girl, Hillview)

While teachers emphasised the importance of being an authoritative figure for the children, they also wanted to be perceived by them as being kind and fair. Developing a positive relationship with the children was seen to be an important aspect of their role, providing support and guidance as children progressed through the school:

> It would be important to me that I would feel I would have a good relationship with the children... and I would hope they would perceive me as someone who is fair, a friend and can have a laugh with... it would be important to me that I would be there for them to help them with their little worries (Grade 2 teacher, Churchfield)

> I would like them to perceive me as an adult who was fair, kind and who can be stern when necessary (Grade 5 teacher, Hill-view)

That teachers are mostly successful in this regard is evident from the fact that a majority of children (60%), but especially the younger ones, agreed that their teacher was kind to them. However over half the proportion of older children (52%) said they would like to be more popular with their teachers, suggesting that these children would like to have more positive relations with their teachers than they perhaps presently enjoy.

A finding that consistently emerges from the data, then, is the difference between older and younger children in how they perceive their social relations with their teachers. Such differences centred on the perception that teachers were stricter with older children and made greater demands upon them both to work harder and behave 'responsibly':

> In infants the teachers don't get so cross but once you go into first on they get much crosser because the infants aren't quite used to the rules of the school yet but when you are older you are supposed to know (Grade 2 girl, Churchfield)

> The teachers are much nicer to the younger children but as you get older they expect you to be more responsible... they give us work and expect us to do it on our own (Grade 5 boy, Hillview)

Interviews with teachers confirmed that their orientation to children differed as they got older. Among the reasons for the change in relations they cited: pressure of schoolwork, peer relations and a growing defensiveness with adults:

> The children in grade 2 just tell you their whole life story when they're younger whereas in grade 5 they only tell you what they want you to know... they see you more as an adult whereas for the younger children you are nearly a mother to them (Grade 5 teacher, Churchfield)

> I think there is more of a distance there... you are giving them more work, authority. I don't think the younger ones associate you so much with work, more with the person you are. As they get older they become more conscious of their peers and that's where the conditional thing comes in... if they get into trouble a lot of their embarrassment comes from the fact that others are looking at them and not that they are in trouble with an adult but are on the spot in front of other children (Grade 2 teacher, Hillview)

Although teachers and pupils express some dissatisfaction about aspects of their relationship with one another, the emotional climate in each classroom is something that most children appear positively disposed to. In the busy and often pressured environment of the classroom, children generally perceive their teachers to be kind and caring and wanted to have a positive relationship with them. Similarly, the data indicates that teachers seek to have a good working and social relationship with the children in their care. The finding that older children would like to have a more positive relationship with their teachers is interesting in that it suggests that their consistently more negative perception of pupil/teacher relations cannot be explained in developmental terms, by their age alone. It can also be understood in terms of the increasing workloads placed on older children as the requirements of entry to second level schooling and subsequently the adult labour market increasingly come to the fore. This necessitates greater discipline and control over pupil behaviour, compromising the more personal and affective dimension typical of such relations in the junior classes. Children's relationships with one another become an increasingly important aspect of their strategies in coping with such increased regulation and control.

Children's perspectives on their relations with peers and the exercise of power

This is where issues concerning popularity and status come to the fore, as well as the empowerment and oppression of children through interaction with one another.[4] Peers are important in providing release from the constant demands teachers make in the classroom. This is where child culture serves to mediate or offset the tension which builds up through constant adult surveillance. This section details questionnaire and interview data related to these areas, emphasising two distinct but interrelated themes: patterns of power and control in peer relations, and the nature of childhood friendships.

Perceptions of power and control in peer relations

The centrality of peer relations to children's social lives is evident from how many children (72%) identified a child rather than an adult as having the most power in school. From a child's perspective, having power implied being big and strong, a member of a gang, clever/knowledgeable and a teacher's pet. Perceptions of those with the least power followed a similar pattern, with an emphasis on children perceived to be physically weak. Interview data confirmed these patterns:

> Anthony is the most powerful cos he has a gang... everybody is afraid of them and they are not afraid of anybody (Grade 5 boy, Churchfield)

> Grade 6 have the most power cos they are the biggest and the strongest (Grade 2 boy, Parkway)

> The babies have the least power cos they're younger... they haven't done what we have done... they don't know percentages in maths like what we've done an that... they've only done 'plus' and 'takeaway'... and they don't know their words (Grade 5 girl, Hillview)

The interviews also indicated that power in children's minds was firmly linked to popularity (arising in particular from sporting and/ or academic ability, as well as the capacity to be tough), with the accompanying capacity to influence others:

> We're the most popular people in the class... cos every one knows us... they think we're mad an we're the best foot-ballers... if there was a fight between our class and a different class the ringleaders would be us (Grade 5 boys, Parkway)

> Tina's very good at her Irish and her Art and everybody really likes her (Grade 2 girl, Churchfield)

> I'd like to be like Joan Costelloe... cos everybody thinks she is the best... cos she acts tough... It's not that I'd like to be tough it's just that everybody likes her... I think nearly everybody is afraid of her (Grade 5 girl, Parkway)

While being considered clever at school was also an important source of popularity, such cleverness had to be managed carefully. Children were anxious not to be perceived as too much of a 'goody goody':

> We don't want to do our work the minute the teacher goes out cos then we'd be goody two shoes (Grade 2 girl, Churchfield)

> You have to keep up your reputation... you can't be a goody goody either... like always telling and always getting your work right, asking questions, not breaking the rules (Grade 5 boy, Churchfield)

Such comments indicate that popularity and status among children often stems from the degree to which they are prepared to challenge adult norms and expectations[5]. An important rule in child culture is not 'telling tales', and this ensures that much of children's behaviour that would be frowned upon by adults remains hidden from them. 'Not telling' appears to be part of a bonding process between children, with diminished popularity and status for those who break this unspoken rule:

> say he did something really bad in the yard... well we wouldn't tell on him but he would tell on us... the teachers just stick up for him cos he doesn't have many friends (Grade 5 boy, Churchfield)

> sometimes the children say: 'If you don't tell on me I won't tell
> on you' and then the teacher never finds out... the children
> make an agreement (Grade 2 girl, Churchfield)

Interview data revealed elements of bullying, for example, which remained firmly within the boundaries of the children's world because
of children's reluctance to 'tell', a finding noted in other research
related to the experience of bullying in Irish schools (O'Moore and
Minton, 2003). Children's comments indicate some of the incidents
involved:

> The hardest thing about being a child at school is sometimes
> it's hard to get a better deal... like you get a bad deal swapping
> things... it's like bullying really... some children are afraid to
> come to school (Grade 5 boy, Churchfield)

> Anto owes me about 50p now... I just give him the money cos
> he keeps on and on about it... he knows it works... he boxed me
> real hard the other day and he was only messing but it hurts
> (Grade 5 girl, Parkway)

An issue that emerged in many of the interviews was the competition
for status between fifth and grade 6 children, both boys and girls –
often resolved by fights. This was evident in observational data in
the three schools and, in addition, children in Hillview engaged in a
ritual called 'beatins' at the start of each year:

> At the start of the year there was fights goin on with Grade 5
> beatins... Grade 6 all gang up and they all start fighting with
> Grade 5... inside and outside the school... the teachers don't
> really know the proper word for it... they might be suspicious
> that something is going on ..they know Grade 6 think they are
> a lot bigger than Grade 5 but they don't know that they beat
> them up (Grade 5 boy, Hillview)

It is clear then that children are highly sensitive to dynamics of
power in their relations with others in school and strive to attain
popularity and status by being tough, clever or good at something,
particularly sport. While these dynamics operate alongside those between teachers and pupils, they are not fully independent of them.
This is evident in the tendency, for example, of clever children to be
seen as powerful/popular, with the perception of cleverness itself influenced by the manner in which teachers both reward and acknow-

ledge achievement in school. However, the reluctance of children to be seen as 'goody goodies' indicates the attempt in child culture to forge patterns of behaviour which do not totally conform with adult norms and expectations. For children who wish to achieve academically in school, this creates the dilemma of trying to straddle both worlds, appealing to both adult and peer norms. Where power is exercised in an oppressive manner between children, as in the case of bullying, this dilemma is also in evidence: many children are reluctant to tell teachers because they fear lowering their social standing among their peers.

The nature of childhood friendships

Given the crowded and often pressured atmosphere of the school and classroom, being alone without friends can be a terrifying prospect. The importance of friends in helping children to cope in school is evident from the 53% who highlighted supportiveness as being the trait they most liked in their friends. Further traits identified included sharing common interests and being funny. During the course of interviews, it became clear that there were two major categories of friends to which children could belong – best/true friends or friends. The distinction between these categories revolved around issues of trust, loyalty and support, with best friends counted on to display certain characteristics:

> All the grade 6 are always messing and coming over to us and jumping on us... and you don't like it ... so we all made an agreement that if one got punched we'd all punch the other guy cos we are true friends. (Grade 5 boy, Hillview)

> Patricia and myself are not best friends... we are good friends... best friends are loyal to each other... you can tell secrets to them... other friends if you tell them secrets they go around blabbing (Grade 5 girl, Hillview)

Membership of particular groups or gangs was evident in all classes, and each gang was attributed certain traits or characteristics:

> Kate, Sorcha and Doreen... they're kind of a big gang... we're just three in ours... we just muck around together... we're tomboys... we like playing boy's games... things like soccer and rounders... they like playing things like barbies and they bring

their barbies to the yard... we just play with the boys (Grade 2 girls, Churchfield)

Anthony has a gang of George, Noel and Keith... everybody is afraid of them and they are not afraid of anybody... and if somebody is beating up that person they will come in and start killing them (Grade 5 boy, Churchfield)

While being part of a gang is empowering for children in terms of providing a sense of belonging, exclusion and the excluding of others demonstrates the exercise of power in a more negative sense. Through adult eyes, children's friendship groups appear transient and fleeting but for children the boundaries of being allowed in or pushed out of particular groups are firmly laid out:

Sometimes we say nasty things about Cora... but we only do it because she won't get the message that we don't want to play with her today... sometimes we make a deal with her that we will only play with her at little break but not at big lunch but then she won't leave us alone at big lunch... she's jealous you see... she loves Doreen... we stay over at night sometimes and she wants to do that too (Grade 2 girls, Churchfield)

The desire to belong, or the security gained from belonging can influence how children interact with one another, especially the extent to which they will challenge others:

Once we were standing on the table and Kate said to Sorcha: 'Oh look what they are doing!'... and she wanted to tell but she didn't want us to know cos she still wanted to be our friend (Grade 5 girl, Churchfield)

Sometimes the popular people really fall out with one another but they don't care... they know they are popular so they don't mind falling out with someone (Grade 5 boy, Hilview)

The dynamics of children's friendship patterns filtered into all aspects of their school lives. In the classroom, for example, the dynamics of support between friends was crucial when work proved difficult, as children sought to hide their confusion from the teacher:

Marcus spends a lot of the time explaining to Noel how to do the sums. Finally Noel understands and says aloud to the group 'yes! these sums are easy'. When the teacher comes around to the group Noel tells her that the sums are easy. She smiles approvingly. (Observation notes for Grade 5 Churchfield)

Conversely the absence of such support was signalled when children covered their work or set up a wall made from books so that their neighbours could not copy. Teasing others about incorrect work was also common ('thicko', 'dumbo'), particularly among the children in grade 5 in Churchfield, but this was always out of the earshot of the teacher. Sharing school materials such as pencils, rulers etc was a further marker of friendship, as was swapping prized possessions (football figurines, pop group memorabilia). Disputes over ownership of such items frequently led to children falling out with one another, changing alliances within peer groups. Boys frequently sought status among friends by having a laugh at the expense of teachers. The following excerpt from field notes records a typical example:

> Teacher: 'I want nothing but the best from you in your sentences. You'll need your atlas to help you. Anthony can you give me a sentence with Holland in it?'
>
> Anthony: 'Hash is legal in Holland'
>
> *The teacher ignores Anthony's response and moves to another child. All the children laugh.* (Observation notes for grade 5, Churchfield)

Break time provided children with the best opportunity to have fun in school. The schoolyards, though rather bleak and barren, resonated with the sound of shouting children. While they may be critical of the space allocated to them for playing in (see Chapter 4), it is in the schoolyard that children have some freedom from adult control and where child culture can flourish. Children's sense of liberation during playtime is evident not only from the screeches and the rush to get to the yard first, but also from their awareness that teachers find it impossible to keep an eye on all that happens there:

> Sometimes there does be a big crowd and everyone gathers around and the teacher does be saying get away get away and the loser is hopped on... if the other fella gets totally wrecked in the fight everybody just hops on him ... it's for fun... normally you see the teacher doesn't really catch them cos when the

> teacher comes over they shout 'sketch' and they all run away
> and the teacher is trying to find out who did it and doesn't un-
> less someone tells... mostly children say :'Oh I didn't see it'
> (Grade 5 boy, Hillview)

Observational data confirmed that teachers on supervision duty circled the playgrounds, trying to keep some order in the apparent chaos. Some seemed more strict than others, isolating children who were caught fighting or, in the case of Hillview, recording their names in a notebook. Mostly, however, children's behaviour went unchecked – the yard was their space and they interacted freely within it. Free from the glare of adult eyes, a world of 'backstage' (Giddens, 1984; Goffman, 1971) behaviour abounded that consisted of fights, 'rude rhymes' and the use of 'bad' language:

> We have lots of scraps in the yard cos children are calling one
> another names like Dickhead and Wanker... no way would we
> say them in front of the teacher (Grade 5 boy, Churchfield)

> Vote vote vote for De Valera,
> In comes Katie at the door eye oh,
> Where is the one with the pimple on her bum,
> We don't want Katie anymore...
> that's the rude one but we stop singing it when the teacher
> comes along or if there was someone we didn't like we'd sing
> the rude one (Grade 5 girl, Churchfield)

It would be a mistake to assume, however, that the only fun children had in the yard consisted of deviant or anti-authoritarian behaviour. Most of the children's time was taken up with playing games. These varied with the time of the year and were largely distinguishable on the basis of age and gender, mirroring the findings of other studies (e.g Blatchford, 1989; Barnett, 1988; Lodge and Flynn, 2001; Thorne, 1993). Chasing games were common for all (despite the no running rule in each yard) but grade 5 boys, in particular those in Hillview and Churchfield, had a robbers and jail game which they played consistently. Some girls joined in occasionally (the 'tom-boys'), but they mostly busied themselves playing rhyming games, walking around in twos and threes and, in Parkway, minding the 'babies'. As identified in other research, the schoolyard was an important space in which children's gender identity was formed and confirmed (Grugeon, 1993; Lodge and Flynn, 2001). Whatever activities children engaged in, it was clear that each game had its own series of rules, well understood and rehearsed by the participants:

> I play with the babies, we play Mammies and Daddies, black and white... if you stand on the white line your on (Grade 2 girl, Parkway)

> We play the den... that's playing chasing on the lines of the basketball courts and you are safe if you are in the middle (Grade 5 boy, Hillview)

The data suggests that friendship groups are a central aspect of children's school experience, providing some relief from the challenges and difficulties posed by the academic and social aspects of their school lives. A clear hierarchy exists in the children's friendship patterns, with specific norms in place that distinguish best friends from friends. While being part of a friendship group is empowering, the need for friends can be a double-edged sword, particularly where children are excluded from a friendship group and find themselves at the lower end of the friendship hierarchy.

Concluding comments

In exploring social relations in school we can return to the three central questions posed in chapter one:

1. How do the children experience social relations with their teachers?

2. What does their experience tell us about the exercise of power between adults and children and the structuring of childhood through school?

3. In what way do children exercise agency through their social relations in school?

The analysis presented in this chapter suggests that in their relations with their teachers, children prioritise the manner in which the teacher interacts with them (by being kind, polite, happy, patient) as much as their teaching skills. While the children enjoyed positive relations with their teachers and generally perceived them to be kind and caring, this was overshadowed for older children by the absence of consultation over much of their experience in school. Issues related to fairness in the allocation of punishments, schoolwork and special jobs emerged in their criticisms as well as a sense that teachers did not take their views seriously on matters that concerned them. Younger children saw being a teacher as being in charge and generally accepted their subordinate position to teachers.

The findings indicate that children see themselves as subordinate to adults in the school. The locus of power is communicated primarily through the ability of teachers, by virtue of their adult status, to 'boss' children and control their time and space. Through the patterning of relations between teachers and pupils in school, childhood is structured as a period of compliance and subordination for the greater good of education and learning. Such compliance, however, operates in a social context of support, praise and encouragement with, as we see in Chapter 5, the use of rewards to overcome resistance to such control. Acceptance of this patterning of child/adult relations is predicated on children's perception of the longterm value of their education. Accordingly, middle class children are least likely in practice to resist teacher control in the classroom, in spite of their greater assertion in interviews of their right to exercise a voice in school. Thus children who possess the cultural capital (Bourdieu, 1993) to know and actively play the system choose to accept the patterning of child/adult relations in school. Those who do not subscribe to such long-term ideals, such as the working class boys in Parkway, actively resist teacher authority through daily inattentiveness and misbehaviour.

Observational and interview data confirmed the importance teachers placed on maintaining control in the pupil/teacher relationship. While every teacher demonstrated a strong commitment to care for the children in their classrooms, generally they had little conscious appreciation of the need to consult and engage with children in a structured way about their experience of school. Such views may be understandable in terms of the time and resource pressures on teachers (in themselves indicative of broader influences related to the under resourcing of primary school education). However, teachers' own belief systems regarding the nature of children and childhood must also be considered. The findings suggest that such systems are framed in terms of child-centred discourse, which advocates sensitivity to children but can leave traditional hierarchical relations between adults and children intact. At the senior level of primary school, this is further reinforced by the increased workload placed on grade 5 children, with the more personal dynamic that characterises interactions with younger children being replaced by a more instrumental and disciplined approach with the older children. This is further explored in Chapter 3 in relation to the experience of the curriculum.

Schools are spaces that are primarily controlled and defined by adults. Children are constantly evaluated in terms of productivity, efficiency and competitiveness, their identities defined and re-defined with reference to adult norms. However, children also evaluate and control one another in their own social world: one that is free from adult surveillance and control. Through their immersion in child culture children not only explore the boundaries of their emerging personal and social identities but also regain a sense of autonomy and control in their relations with their teachers. In this sense they are agents, undermining adult authority through their collective emphasis on play and games at every available opportunity they get in school. While the schoolyard provides the ultimate space in which children participate in this world, there are other spaces too. The toilets, corridors, under the desks, at the back of the classroom, putting rubbish in the bin – all provide opportunities for the children to side-step teacher demands for compliance and learning. Though children may perceive their relations with teachers to be a matter of subordination and control, such control is never complete, undermined as it is by children's capacities as active agents to resist outright domination. As the school year unfolds, teachers and pupils come to a shared understanding of what is and what is not tolerated in their interactions with one another. Negotiating is an important aspect of the exercise of power between teachers and pupils in school.

Notes

1 These findings coincide with those of a recent study in Irish post-primary schools (Lynch and Lodge, 2002) where students repeatedly voiced their concerns over the perceived absence of respect by teachers for their views and perspectives on aspects of school life.

2 This is a good example of the control exercised over the physical body alluded to by Foucault (1979) as discussed in Chapter 7.

3 The term 'bold' in an Irish context means 'naughty'.

4 While this study did not examine in detail the issue of bullying, other research in the field highlights its prevalence as a form of interaction between young people in school. A nationwide study (O'Moore, Kirkham and Smith, 1997) indicated that 31.3% of primary school children between the ages of eight and twelve reported being bullied at school. In a later study, O'Moore and Minton (2003) indicated children were very reluctant to report being bullied owing to a fear of being further bullied and being labelled a 'tell tale'. Not telling is an important social rule in child culture.

5 For further discussion of this in relation to children's attitudes to school rules see also Chapter 5.

3

Power and the Curriculum:
Children's Perspectives

Introduction

The primary school curriculum is devised and implemented by adults, and reflects their concerns and priorities in the education of children. It provides a framework within which they organise the time and space of children in school. Whether children experience the curriculum as oppressive or empowering is an important indicator of the exercise of power between adults and children. In his analysis, Bernstein (1975) directly relates curricular experience to pupil's rights and status, and maintains that a centralised, subject centred curriculum is one which decreases pupils' status, hence their rights, in school. Arguably, the nature of the curriculum may also constrain or empower teachers as they implement societal demands for specific forms of learning through their classroom practice. Research in the area of children's experience of the curriculum suggests that while most children favour subjects such as Physical Education and Art, their experience of and attitude toward the curriculum is not static and is often influenced by factors such as student gender, social class and age (McCallum, *et al*, 2000; Pollard and Triggs, 2000, Pollard, Thiessen and Filer, 1997; Tizard *et al*, 1988). The public context of school learning also ensures that children's attitudes toward their learning in the subject areas will be influenced by their perception of their abilities in each area, shaping their preferences for certain subjects. Research also indicates that children become increasingly instrumental in their orientation to the curriculum as they become older, highlighting the manner in which they internalise adult discourse on the purpose and role of school (Christensen and James, 2001; Cullingford, 1991; King, 1989; Pollard and Triggs, 2000; Woods, 1990).

This chapter details children's and teachers' perception of and attitudes toward the school curriculum[1]. It focuses on children's likes and dislikes of school subjects. What the children view as being the most and least important school subjects are juxtaposed with the teachers' attitudes toward the curriculum. This is followed by an analysis of how children actually experience the curriculum on a daily basis.

What children say about the curriculum

When examining the children's attitudes toward the curriculum I noted two specific areas: the preferences children displayed for some subjects over others and the importance they attributed to some forms of learning over others in school.

Subjects the children liked best

The children were asked to rank the subjects they liked most. Below are the four subjects which received the highest combined first and second preference scores:

Table 3.1 Children's subject preference by age level and gender

Subject	Junior	Senior	Girls	Boys	% total who gave this their first preference:
Art	26	19	36	20	27
PE	25	41	21	46	31
Sums	13	7	19	10	14
English	23	6	9	11	11

Note: Figures given are percentages out of a sample total of 133 children.

Subjects children most favoured included Physical Education and Art, followed by 'Sums'. English (Reading and Writing), Music and History (for the older children only) were mentioned more in second choice preferences. Significant gender and age differences were identified (P<.01 and P<.001 respectively) with boys and older children most likely to express a preference for PE and girls and younger children a preference for Art. The greater overall value placed on Physical Education is also supported by the fact that over one third of the children, particularly the younger children and boys, cited this subject as the best thing about coming to school.

When the older children were asked to specify why they preferred certain subjects over others[2], they tended to focus on the degree of fun and interest involved and whether they perceived themselves as good at the subject. (See Table 3.2 below). These findings mirror those of Pollard and Triggs (2000), in the emphasis placed on ease, fun and interest in determining subject preferences. In particular, Physical Education and Art were chosen as the subjects most liked because they were fun, while 'Sums' tended to be chosen by children who perceived themselves to be good at them:

Table 3.2: Reasons for preferred subject (open question)

Reason	N	%
I'm good at it	13	17.1
It's fun	31	40.7
It's interesting	19	25.0
It's not really work	5	6.5
Missing	8	10.5
Totals	76	100.0

Interviews with children of all age groups supported these findings, reflected in the comments below:

> The subjects I like most are maths cos I'm good at it, PE cos it's fun and religion cos there's a good story (grade 5 boy, Churchfield)

> I actually like Irish... but nobody believes me when I say that... but I do (grade 5 girl, Hillview)

In their talk, younger children emphasise the freedom of expression and movement offered in subjects such as Art and Physical Education. They also identify excitement at learning new and interesting things as a positive attribute of particular subjects:

> I like doing art and PE 'cos in PE you can run around the hall and play and in Art you can slap around the paint on pictures (grade 2 girl, Parkway)

> I like nature cos you get to know how animals live their lives (grade 2 girl, Churchfield)

Liking a subject can also derive from the pleasure felt in completing learning:

> I like reading and sums... your teacher calls you up to do your reading and when you do loads of pages you get to finish the book... (grade 2 girl, Parkway)

There were subjects which the children did not like, however, and these are listed in rank order in Table 3.3 below:

Table 3.3 Children's least favoured subjects

Subject	Junior	Senior	Girl	Boy	% total who gave this their least preference
Irish	27	31	25	34	30
Sums	22	17	23	16	20
English	16	5	10	10	10
Geography	–	12	8	8	7
History	–	12	7	4	4

Note: Figures given are percentages, out of a total sample of 133 children

The subjects the children liked least included Irish, 'sums' and English, with Geography and History[3] also listed among the responses of the older children. Significant gender differences were noted ($P<.05$), with girls more likely to dislike sums and boys to dislike Irish. The differences in responses between older and younger children in relation to English (reading and writing) is noteworthy and may reflect the particular challenge this area poses to children in their early years of schooling, as commented upon by other researchers in the field (Pollard and Triggs, 2000; Tizard *et al*, 1988). In general children's ability level (based on the children's own rankings of their ability) did not significantly influence attitudes toward curricular subjects, although those who identified themselves as 'not so clever' were more inclined to express a preference for PE and to emphasise 'hardness' as the reason why they disliked certain subjects. As children's ability ranking increased, a more instrumental orientation was evident in their dislike of certain subjects. Children who perceived themselves to be 'very clever' were most likely to state they disliked a subject (P<.05) because it was irrelevant or they didn't need it for their future working lives.

The preferences and dislikes indicated by the children reflect the priority they place on having fun as well as engaging in work which does not threaten their vulnerability as learners in the classroom. This latter is borne out by the most frequent reasons the children give for not liking certain subjects (Table 3.4): too hard or boring. Pollard and Triggs (2000) note however that labelling a subject as 'boring' can have many different meanings, including a perception that the subject is too hard or too easy.

Table 3.4: Reasons for not liking subjects

Reasons	N	%
It's too hard	28	36.8
It's boring	33	43.4
It's irrelevant	6	7.8
No Answer	9	11.8
Totals	76	100.0

Irish was chosen as the subject children least liked[4] primarily because it was perceived as hard (58% expressed this view) or boring (31%) while those who chose 'sums' as their least preferred subject perceived it to be too hard.

Comments that children made during the course of interviews emphasise the difficulty of particular subjects, the amount of repetition in learning and the perceived irrelevance of some subjects to the immediacy of their lives:

I don't like doing Irish cos it's a different language and I don't know how to do it and I have to work really hard at it... every time she says take out your Irish book we all say aw! (grade 2 boy, Churchfield)

I don't like Maths cos I can never add up numbers in my head... I never could, I hate nature cos who cares where the badger lives, geography cos why learn about other countries if you don't live in them (grade 5 girl, Hillview)

Perceptions of the importance of curricular subjects

When asked to outline the subjects they considered most important, the children identified English, 'sums' and Irish. This is not surprising given that such subjects can account in practice for up to 65% of the total timetable (Hayes and Kernan, 2001), more than matching DES specifications that they should account for 55% of school time (NCCA, 1990)[5]. As Table 3.5 indicates, younger children were more likely to stress the importance of English (reading and writing) and sums, while their older counterparts emphasised sums (P<.05).

Table 3.5 Children's rankings by importance

Subject	Junior	Senior	% total who ranked this subject as most important:
Sums	33	40	38
English (Reading/Writing)	38	18	27
Irish	16	20	18

Children's perception of the relative importance of some subjects over others draws on an adult oriented discourse of preparation for work and adult life in general. Needing a subject to get a job ('sums' and Irish were most often identified in these terms) or for life in general (English was more commonly defined in this way) was indicated in the responses of older children (see Table 3.6).

The least important subjects, as all the children saw things, reinforces this instrumentalist orientation to school learning. Art activities, Physical Education and Music were defined as least important (see Table 3.7).

Table 3.6 Reasons why subject is important

Reason why subject is important	N	%
Need it for a job	24	31.5
Need it for life	34	44.7
Need it for Secondary School	4	5.2
We do it a lot in school	3	3.9
No Answer	11	14.7
Totals	76	100.0

Table 3.7 Children's perception of the least important subjects

Subject	Junior	Senior	% Total who ranked this subject as least important:
Art	17	32	20
PE	23	21	17
Music	8	15	11

Note: Figures are in percentages, out of a total sample of 133 children.

When the older grade 5 children were asked to give reasons for their chosen rankings, the linkage drawn between the importance of a subject and the level of work (as opposed to fun) involved is particularly evident, as noted in Table 3.8 below:

Table 3.8: Reasons why subject is thought unimportant

Reason why least important	N	%
It's not really work	26	34.4
I can learn it at home	8	10.5
We don't do it much	5	6.5
We don't need it for work/life	4	5.2
No answer	14	18.4
Totals	76	100.0

The table reveals that grade 5 children are very clear about what they consider as real work in school, discounting subjects such as Art, Physical Education and Music. Some children rated them as least important because they could learn them at home. This suggests that for these children the school curriculum is just that – learning which takes place only in the school environment and which is needed for adult working life.

Comments during the course of interviews with the entire cohort of children reinforced how instrumental children's orientation toward the school curriculum was:

> I think he wants us to work our hardest at sums cos you wouldn't get into third level college with out them (grade 2 girl, Churchfield)

> Art, Music and PE are the least important because they don't include brainwork... you can't get a job with those subjects (grade 5 girl, Parkway)

The children's views appeared to be influenced by the teachers' own attitudes toward the subject, conveyed by the amount of time spent doing it or by the teacher's reaction to the effort children put in to learning:

> I think maths is the most important cos if you get loads wrong the teacher gets really mad and if you get loads right the teacher will be really nice (grade 2 girl, Churchfield)

> PE isn't that important cos you are only running around, art as well cos she doesn't get really cross unless the art is for something really important like Holy Communion in the church (grade 2 girl, Parkway)

This demonstrates not only children's sensitivity to teacher mood but also how power is exercised through everyday classroom practice, such practice communicating to children the relative value of some forms of learning and intelligences (Gardner, 1997) over others in school. Children understand what is valued not only by the positioning of subjects on the timetable but also by the way teachers behave and react towards them on the basis of their schoolwork. The working of the timetable itself was also an issue – a central instrument in the control of the time-space paths of children. The children expressed the view that they would like greater balance between work time and playtime in the organisation of their activities in school. Understood in the context of the exercise of power between adults and children, what these children are arguing for is a marrying of the worlds of adult and child so that the priorities of each group are given equal weight in the school day:

> we should be allowed choose about PE or going out to the yard... we'd mix work and play more... like at the beginning of the year we could decide the timetable and have an hour of work and an hour break (grade 5 girl, Churchfield)

The fact that teachers could choose to do the subjects they liked irritated the children, highlighting their lack of choice in such matters:

> teachers sort of choose the subjects they like... so they do that a lot... like our teacher loves Irish or when we had nuns they did a lot of religion (grade 5 girl, Churchfield)

They also express particular annoyance at the routine nature of the timetable and the fact that the hardest subjects seem to be put first:

> She picks all the hard things first... like the worst things... the bad things like Irish... to get them out of the way... and she loves Irish herself (grade 5 boy, Churchfield)

The children's comments reflect their desire to cater for child culture as well as adult expectations for learning in the organisation of the timetable, to balance children's love of fun and freedom with the 'real work' of Irish, English and mathematics.

Experiencing the curriculum in practice

The analysis has shown that children have specific preferences and dislikes, as well as a clear understanding of what is important and what is not. However, the interview data also highlights the pressure children feel that working through particular aspects of the curriculum puts on them, not only because of the quantity of work they must cover, but also because of the time allowed to do it in. The older children in the study felt this pressure most.

> Children aren't allowed to sit together cos they talk and they have a lot of work to do... but twenty minutes to do fifty sums... I don't think that's fair... (grade 5 girl, Churchfield)

> Some teachers don't understand what it's like... how hard it is... like they might say do the next six questions and they might be the hardest in the book... and twenty minutes later they say have you got them all done even though they would take half an hour... if they had to be children for just one day they would know it was hard and find out what it was like to do a question in five minutes... or get extra homework (grade 5 boy, Hillview)

In many ways the views of children parallel those of teachers in the study. Senior class teachers in all three schools spoke of the competitive nature of the system, the intensification of their teaching role (Hargreaves, 1998, 1994) and the overly academic and pressured nature of their teaching work:

> I think in the senior classes you are more aware of the pressures... but that's the way the system is and I can't change it on my own (grade 5 teacher, Parkway)

> It seems to filter down from university... academic subjects dictate what the curriculum will be in secondary school and then primary school... You feel if you don't do so much now they will lose out when they go to secondary school (grade 5 teacher, Hillview)

> The textbooks... they are very big and heavy and when you consider there are only 183 days in the school year and you are trying to fit in every subject... they learn very little for practical life... to be responsible for themselves (grade 5 teacher, Churchfield)

In contrast, the curriculum for younger children was perceived by all the teachers interviewed to be less pressurised, allowing greater flexibility and freedom in its implementation. Phrases such as 'drumming in' and 'ploughing through' were typically used to describe the implementation of the grade 5 programme (particularly with respect to the core subjects of mathematics and Irish), whereas fun, play and flexibility were most often mentioned with respect to teaching younger children. While there is an obvious cost to children in terms of their experience of the school day, teachers also felt that they had to compromise on what they considered to be important and of real value in education:

> I would love to spend more time doing music, art and drama... this is my first time having fifth in a long time and you automatically have to take on a different role cos suddenly it's very very serious and a lot of the fun is gone out of it... you have to start drumming into them... especially in maths... I wouldn't like to be at this end of the school for too long (grade 5 teacher, Hillview)

A further source of pressure for both teachers and children alike, albeit from differing perspectives, emerged in relation to the assignment of homework. During the course of interviews, children complained bitterly about homework, viewing it as an unfair intrusion into their private lives, and one over which they had little control. Indeed for many children, homework epitomised the powerful position of the teacher in being able to use it as a form of punishment, as well as extending their surveillance (Foucault, 1979) beyond the school:

> Homework is bad cos we work hard every day... and then you are sent home to do more... teachers give children homework to keep them occupied... after school you are supposed to go home and relax... not do more homework... it's like the teacher is still there watching you even though you are at home... the only way you get out of it is if you are sick (grade 5 boy, Hillview)

> Sometimes you might not finish your work if it was hard or something and she says: 'ah you've been doing nothing all day'... you have to finish it at home... she does it just to punish you (grade 5 boy, Churchfield)

So while children then were critical of teacher surveillance through the assignment of homework (and some actively resisted by continually forgetting homework copies), teachers themselves felt judged and monitored in terms of the homework they assigned. This was especially the case in the more middle class schools, highlighting the significance of social class in the implementation of the primary curriculum. In middle class Churchfield for example, teachers spoke of how they were pressed to push the children academically, epitomised in giving children 'adequate' homework:

> The children here are very conscious of doing well... I was put under huge pressure by parents to give them homework... I wasn't giving them any written homework... just reading and spellings and they put me under fierce pressure to give them written homework and I was furious... (grade 2 teacher, Churchfield)

> To me homework isn't that important at all...it's more a discipline than anything else... but parents want homework... it's only because of that that I give it (grade 5 teacher, Churchfield)

What is at issue here are competing discourses among adults (in this instance parents and teachers) over the appropriate use of children's time. Such discourses are strongly influenced by social class and the expectations for the children's future achievement in the adult world. The experience of being monitored is not only confined to children, however: teachers themselves comment on homework being used to illustrate to parents the work the teacher is doing in school:

> Half the time when you are giving homework... it's because you are aware that the parent's perception of what the teacher is like is only through homework or the only reflection of what they might get at home of what is happening in class (grade 2 teacher, Hillview)

In Parkway however, a school with designated disadvantaged status, such pressure from parents was absent and this, coupled with a reluctance by teachers to overburden the children academically, created a less pressurised approach to the implementation of the school curriculum[6]:

> Here the parents would rarely question what you do with the children... they just want them to be happy (grade 2 teacher, Parkway)

> We're lucky here in that we wouldn't have the pressure of getting things done... we're quite flexible... you don't feel you have to have all the books done before passing the children on... so there's no rigidly holding you through the programme (grade 5 teacher, Parkway)

Children themselves can put pressure on one another over the curriculum. Aspects of child culture related to the maintenance of status by finishing first, or getting work done correctly, can exacerbate the vulnerability some children may already feel in tackling their work at school:

> There is competition between children in the class... one girl always rushes her work and tries to get up to the teacher first and says: 'I'm finished'... it's stupid... and she copies... that's why she gets full marks... last year I was quite fast at my work but now I don't mind... I just try and get through it... (grade 5 girl, Churchfield)

Once again social class appears to be an important influential factor here, with middle class children more likely to compete on these terms than their working class counterparts. Owing to Parkway's policy of not placing the children under undue academic pressure, competition between children in terms of their academic achievement did not appear as an issue of concern in the interviews.

Concluding remarks

Returning to the three questions I set out in chapter one, the children's comments indicate a mixed experience of the curriculum and that their perspectives are shaped by the levels of interest, fun and ease in each school subject. Children consistently expressed a preference for subjects such as Art and Physical Education, while subjects such as mathematics, English and Irish were least liked. The data also indicates that children experience the curriculum primarily as a form of work, and perceive certain subjects such as Art and Physical Education a release from the concentrated learning demanded in subjects such as Irish, English and mathematics. This was particularly the case for older mainly middle class children, who spoke of their curricular experiences in terms of the pressure to complete tasks quickly and correctly. These were also the children who complained most about the extension of school work to the domain of their home lives through the allocation of homework.

In terms of the exercise of power between adults and children it is clear that the more adult-centred goals of productivity and longterm usefulness inform children's perception of what is valued and considered as 'real' learning in their curricular experience. Such values are communicated to the children not only through the length of time allocated to different subjects, but also through the perceived seriousness with which teachers treat learning in certain subject areas. The absence of consultation with children over what they learn, along with the relative imbalance between playtime and work time reinforces a perception of schooling as something which is done to the children, with little cognisance of their priorities for fun, games and play. The selection of some areas of learning over and above others and the time prioritised for specific areas of learning is a key element in the exercise of power in educational systems.[7] A central component of this power is the structuring of childhood in a manner which gives precedence to instrumental goals over those related for example to personal, social and artistic development.

Interviews with teachers confirmed the instrumental thrust of the school curriculum. They also pointed to the teachers' own frustrations with the restrictions this placed upon them in fulfilling a more broadly based educative role. While a revised curriculum that includes a greater emphasis on social and artistic development is currently being phased into primary schools, findings by Hayes and Kernan (2001) confirm the tendency noted previously (NCCA, 1990; INTO, 1985; O'Sullivan, 1980) for teachers to emphasise the core areas of reading, writing and mathematics in their teaching. Greater availability of inservice education for teachers[8] as well as prioritising the funding of primary education through reduced class sizes may go some way to counteract more conservative tendencies in the implementation of the curriculum. However, from the children's perspective, the prioritisation of 'work' over 'play' in the organisation of their learning signals the primary role of schooling as preparation for adult life and the accompanying need for discipline and concentration in school.

In spite of such restraints, however, children's agency is also evident in their experience of the curriculum. In applying themselves on a daily basis to the demands of learning, children draw on a wide range of academic and social skills. These include perseverance in the face of learning tasks, especially those which are perceived to be 'hard' or 'boring' while simultaneously juggling status oriented pressures within their peer group to be first, fast and right in the completion of assignments. It must also be stressed that it is through children's agency – their school labour (Qvortrup, 1987 and 2001) as they engage daily with the demands of the curriculum, that the long term adult goals of economic development and productivity prevail.

Notes

1 Note that the research was conducted prior to the phased introduction of the Revised Primary Curriculum (1999). While this places a greater emphasis than heretofore on social and artistic development, the core emphasis on subjects such as English, Irish and mathematics remains.

2 Responses to this area were yielded through a questionnaire. Some areas were not included in the questionnaires devised for the younger cohort due to the need for brevity and simplicity but these children's views were ascertained on this aspect of curricular experience during the course of the interviews.

3 History and Geography are introduced to children for the first time in third class when they are typically nine years old.

4 For an interesting account of young people's attitudes toward the learning and speaking of Irish see Nic Ghiolla Phádraig (2001).

5 Under the revised Primary Curriculum (1999) a minimum of four hours of weekly instruction is recommended for English language instruction and three hours each for Irish, mathematics, social environmental and scientific education (a new curricular area) and Arts education (to include Visual arts, music and drama). Physical Education is to be allocated a minimum of one hour per week, Social and Personal Health education thirty minutes (a new curricular area) and teachers have a two hours discretion curriculum time. It is also worth noting that two hours and thirty minutes out of a total weekly attendance of twenty eight hours is allocated to recreation time.

6 The influence of social class on teacher expectations for pupil learning is well documented in the literature (e.g. Anyon, 1981; Conway, 2002; MacRuaric, 1997; Means, Chelemer and Knapp, 1991; Oakes and Lipton, 1999; O'Sullivan, 1984).

7 For a fuller discussion of the sociology of knowledge and the selective tradition in curricular organisation see for example classic texts by Young (1970) and Apple (1979).

8 Criticisms over the lack of appropriate inservice education for teachers with the introduction of the curriculum in 1970 has given rise to a structured framework of school-based inservice for all teachers in the phasing in of the Revised Primary Curriculum (1999).

4

Pedagogical Practices
in Schools

Introduction

Where as the curriculum provides the framework within which children's time and space in school is organised, pedagogy is concerned with how learning takes place. Like the curriculum, pedagogy is implicitly tied up with the exercise of power between teachers and pupils – between adults and children – framing children's learning in terms of certain goals and values (Bernstein, 1975, 1990, 1996; Singh, 2002). The concept of pedagogy used here refers to the control which is exercised over the activities of children in the classroom. Time and Space is much emphasised in recent analyses of children's lives (Christensen and James, 2001; Moore and Lackney, 1993; Sampson *et al*, 1999; Zeiher, 2001) and in this chapter a key focus is placed on the organisation of children's space and the level of control exercised over their activity in school. For our purposes, it involves considering the values that are implied by the structure and organisation of classroom space, discipline procedures and the taken for granted rules of classroom behaviour. Through such practices teachers communicate to children the discourses they draw upon related to learning, education and childhood. Previous research in this area highlights the tendency for teachers to exercise considerable control over children's classroom activity and the structuring of school and class-

53

room space to facilitate such control (Campbell, 1998; Darmarin, 1995; Devine, 1991; King, 1978 and 1989; Pollard and Triggs, 2000; Tirri and Poulinatha, 2000).

This chapter begins the analysis of pedagogical perspectives in school. It documents not only observed pedagogical practice in each of the classrooms in the study but also teachers' perspectives on what they do in school. The chapter taps into the values underpinning the teachers' practice and how these are intended to frame pupil experiences and hence in particular ways their childhood. Specific areas of focus include the organisation of classroom space, pedagogical practice and student control and the goals underpinning pedagogical practices. Chapter five provides a full account of the children's perspectives of the organisation of their time and space in school. To set the context for the analysis a brief description of teaching practice in the schools is provided.

Observations of teaching practice

As with other research in this area, my observation in each of the classrooms indicated a predominance of whole class teaching methods with individual instruction given by the teacher where necessary (Dept of Education, 1990; Galton *et al*, 1999; Osborn *et al*, 2000). Group work, where evident, tended to be in the area of reading. Teachers in each of the junior classes and in grade 5 in Parkway conducted reading instruction in this way. In each classroom there was a blend of oral and written work, the latter predominantly based on exercises in written textbooks or completing tasks set by the teacher on the blackboard. Typical lesson periods involved whole class discussion/questions and answers of the topic in hand followed by the setting of a written task or assignment to be completed by the children individually. For the most part children spent their time working at their desks, their freedom of movement restricted mainly to recreation time out in the schoolyard. Nonetheless there was a constant bustle of activity in each classroom as individual children came and went (going to the toilet, on messages, for learning support etc.) throughout the school day.

The organisation of classroom space

Interviews with teachers indicated that they had taken account of certain factors when organising their classrooms: creating a pleasant physical environment for the children, maintaining discipline through specific seating arrangements and the positive public portrayal of themselves through the care and effort evident in the organisation of the classroom. Classroom layout symbolised the values the teachers held and which they sought to instil in the children:

> Once a class is structured, you are going to be structured and so the children will try and imitate you (grade 5 teacher, Hill-view)

> It's important to me that the classroom is colourful and interesting to look at and for the children too... that they feel a sense of ease there, they have a sense of pride in it (grade 2 teacher, Parkway)

Four of the five classrooms in the study were decorated to a high standard, with notice boards brimming with teacher charts and children's art/written work all conveying a sense of order and reasonable neatness. The classroom in grade 5 in Parkway, though spacious, looked somewhat dishevelled and there was little material displayed on the walls. In contrast, grade 2 in the same school was alight with colour, as the teacher filled every available space with the children's artwork. Animal cut-outs hung low from the ceiling and the children clearly enjoyed ducking under them when they walked around the room.

The importance of classroom organisation for the disciplining of the children emerged in the course of teacher interviews. Seating arrangements in terms both of the layout of classroom furniture and the positioning of individual children were designed to control pupil interaction and facilitate learning. Considerations such as the degree of attentiveness of each child or their perceived ability level influenced the teachers' decision as to where children sat[1]:

> Generally if children are friends and are not too disruptive I leave them together but I consciously put somebody who is good beside someone who is weak ... if I see two weak children together I would consciously move them because I don't think they will help one another and I think it's good to put an untidy

> child beside a tidy child so they can look and see 'oh that is a nice way to line up a page' and learn from that (grade 5 teacher, Hillview)

> I would have the bright, the weak, the chatty and the quiet... I try to mix all that... the ones I have close up to me are the ones I need to keep a little extra eye on... maybe the ones I don't want near me I put at the back if they get on my nerves... I mix their ability and their boldness (grade 2 teacher, Churchfield)

Differences in classroom layout were evident in the study. Parkway favoured a formal arrangement in both classrooms of children seated in rows, whereas the children in both classrooms in Churchfield were seated in groups. Children in grade 5 in Hillview were seated in an open square with a small row in the centre. The grade 2 teacher in Parkway shows the linkage between disciplinary considerations and seating arrangements when she says:

> I always felt that when children are seated in groups it is very hard to see what they are doing... unless they are motivated themselves... I suppose I like them to feel that... I sort of am watching them... I emphasise that particularly here because they are so distracted (grade 2 teacher, Parkway)

Placing the teacher's desk at the top of the classroom facing the children reflected this concern with discipline and the need to let children know they were being monitored:

> I have my desk at the top because it's beside the blackboard and I can see all the children but I have had it at the back so the children couldn't see me but I could see them' (grade 2 teacher, Parkway)

Not all teachers held this view. The teacher of grade 2 in Churchfield said that she enjoyed sitting to the side of the children, where she could not see everything that 'was going on':

> The desk was here when I came... I would always have my desk facing the children but then I decided to keep it here because it's a good idea sometimes not to be looking at the children... just to leave them... you know you don't always have to be watching (grade 2 teacher, Churchfield)

When asked to specify what their ideal classroom would be like, all teachers emphasised issues such as space and brightness and the potential to create areas where children could work on their own or in groups:

> I would like bigger rooms... I haven't got room to do things I'd like so I don't bother... like a reading corner... I'd love to have little areas... have the children have space just for chairs, not desks and have desks against walls so they could work there if they needed it and have extra space for art, project work etc. (grade 5 teacher, Parkway)

> My ideal room would have lots of space and cushions for the children to sit on... maybe once a week where they could be comfortable and do what they want (grade 5 teacher, Church-field)

Their comments indicate the extent to which teachers themselves felt constrained within the space they operated in and how the reality of their classroom practice frequently differed from their own ideals. Their ideals suggest that they desired greater freedom and flexibility in the way the classroom was organised and a less restrained pedagogical style for themselves and for their pupils.

Pedagogical practice and pupil control

A central aspect of pedagogy is the control teachers exerted over pupils to ensure that learning takes place. Because the emphasis is on learning, teachers in the study tended to perceive discipline in primarily positive terms and viewed disciplinary procedures as necessary interventions to ensure children behaved in a socially acceptable manner. This is encapsulated by the principal of Parkway:

> Ground rules are laid down so everyone can enjoy them-selves... they know what's expected so that puts an onus of res-ponsibility on them... you have to have a certain code of con-duct because it's good self discipline... if we didn't have that society would be chaos... a certain discipline has to be instilled in children and we have them for eight years and you can instil a lot of discipline into them which will be good for them in the long run (Principal, Parkway)

Teachers in the study had few observable difficulties maintaining discipline, and used common patterns for the maintenance of children's attention in the classroom. These revolved around the use of signal systems to gain order and attention among the pupils, the direct physical control of children in terms of the positioning of their bodies, the teachers' intonation, the physical presence of the teacher and the use of reward and punishment systems to induce compliance and effort to learn. It is useful to describe practice in each area.

Signal systems as a method of control

Signal systems were an important device to obtain immediate attention from the children and were most often used at the beginning and end of the school day and the transitions from one lesson period to another. Typically they involved the use of prayers to start a lesson, instructions given in Irish – the changeover from one language to another indicating the need for children to pay attention and concentrate – and setting time limits for the completion/preparation of a task by counting. For example:

> Right I am counting to five and I expect everyone to be busy ag obair[2]... lets see who's the best grupa..1... 2... 3... 4... 5... *as children frantically organise themselves.* (grade 2, Churchfield)

> Now! Right! I'm going to count to three and anyone who is talking is getting their name on the blackboard (grade 5, Parkway)

Signals used during the course of the day to indicate the teachers' displeasure over the level of noise or attention included tapping on the desk, clapping hands, placing a finger on the mouth, clicking fingers at individual children. Bells and whistles were used in the schoolyard to signal the start and the end of playtime. All these signals were well understood by the children and in most instances evoked the desired effect.

Control of the body

Foucault (1979) emphasises the importance of controlling the body as a particularly modern form of exercising power, conveying clear message systems related to the norms and values influencing institutional practice. Observations in each of the classrooms are filled with examples of control of this kind, as teachers surveilled the bodily position of children to judge how effectively they were concentrating on the task in hand. In all classes teachers made frequent reference to the position of children's heads, as well as comments about sitting up straight, not slouching or criticising children's bodily position if they looked too comfortable:

> It's interesting to see the people who have their heads down working hard – Andrew is doing great work... look at him head down. Alan is doing marvellous work, I can tell by looking at him (grade 2, Parkway)

> Children! Sit up straight. Hands down from your face. Look as if you are awake (grade 5, Churchfield)

> Now I get worried when I see people slouching in their chairs

For children, having their bodies controlled in this way was symbolic of the teachers' power.

Use of voice

Children were also disciplined through the intonation of teachers' voices, by the teachers in fifth class in Churchfield and second class in Parkway using a calm monotone voice and the teacher in grade 5 in Parkway outroaring the children. In all classes, I heard examples of teachers using their voices to show kindness ('Now I'll go around and help anyone who needs it'), concern ('you're leaning too hard on the pencil – it'll make you tired'), delight ('well done'), indignance ('oh look at those two socialising over there!'), dismay ('Oh lord') and sarcasm ('listen, you might hear something'). Indeed it was not unusual to hear a range of such intonations within a short time, as teachers tried to monitor the behaviour of all of the individuals in each class.

Given the greater authority of the teacher in the classroom it is not surprising that teachers appealed to children on the grounds of their own feelings and expected them to empathise with their particular situation and respond positively. Examples of such comments included:

> 'My nerves are close to the edge, please stop'...
> 'I'm really struggling here to keep your attention'...

> 'My poor voice, do you wonder how I stick it?'...

'Now this really annoys me'...

'Teacher gets tired answering all your questions. I have only one head, two arms and two legs. I can't answer all your questions at once'...

'I'm not going to kill myself shouting at you. I have a sore throat'...

Reward and punishment systems

The use of reward and punishment systems was another important strategy that was evident in all the classrooms in the study but particularly in grade 5 in Parkway. That the teacher had only a tenuous hold of control was evident, as she constantly attempted to redraw the boundaries of classroom behaviour (in particular for boys) through a system of rewards based on stars and points[3] for out of school trips to the cinema. The amount of time and energy she devoted maintaining some degree of control ensured that many children, particularly girls, were pretty well invisible throughout the day. The star system was introduced to redress this imbalance somewhat by drawing attention to the quiet and well behaved, with rewards built in for attendance, punctuality, wearing the uniform and being attentive during lessons. The following excerpt from one observation indicates the typical banter over the awarding of stars:

> Teacher: Okay! children on time tomorrow will get a star
> Peter: I didn't get a star for anything today
> Teacher: Excuse me you did! You got one for your uniform. Peter and Andrew lost a point today so they are down to nine points. Now! People who lost points today would want to mind themselves. I'm going to give extra points to whoever has their place nice and tidy without a spec of dust on the floor (grade 5, Parkway)

Stars and points provided identifiable rewards for the children in terms of positive behaviour. Teachers in all schools used praise and encouragement to motivate children towards making greater effort in their learning. Conversely, threats and punishment were used as important negative sanctions in all the classrooms observed. Threats mainly involved having to move children from one position in the classroom to another, extra homework, sending a note home to parents, having to do lines or be kept in during break-time:

'Stop the talking or I'm going to separate you'
'I'm going to have to start putting names on the blackboard'
The next person I catch talking is getting fifty lines'
'Amanda! If you don't settle, I'll send a note home'
'The more you talk the more sums I write'
'Patricia! Next step for you is Mr Monaghan's'

During the observation periods, there was no direct evidence of children receiving punishments but subsequent interviews with the children confirmed that teachers frequently carried out their threats. Indeed, grade 5 children in Churchfield were told that extra homework would be given to any child 'causing trouble' during my field trips to the school!

Physical presence of the teacher

Teachers are physically present to children by virtue of being bigger and use this to discipline and monitor children's behaviour. All teachers in the study enhanced the children's awareness of their presence by using their eyes and by moving in and out of the space the children occupied. Teachers frequently stopped a lesson and stared directly at children who were inattentive. They watched children out of the corners of their eyes while working with others up at the desk. They also moved about the classroom frequently, making it difficult for children to engage in inattentive behaviour. The freedom of movement engaged in by teachers was in stark contrast to the restricted movement and space allowed each individual child. As we shall see in Chapter 5, differences in the capacity for movement in and out of classroom space symbolised for older children the power and status differences between themselves and the teachers. Teachers who had a strong physical presence (particularly evident in grade 2 in Parkway and grade 5 in Churchfield), tended to have less need for more direct forms of control such as shouting, threatening or rebuking the children (evident in grade 5 in Parkway). All teachers, however, were constantly monitoring children's behaviour, even when appearing to be absorbed by another activity.

Goals and values reflected in pedagogical practices[4]

The methods of discipline and control evident in the classrooms observed show high levels of surveillance of children by teachers.

Such discipline and control derived from teacher attachment to particular values and goals in their practice, values which revolved around academic learning, social responsibility and the promotion of positive self-esteem. All teachers expressed the view that they would like the children to be happy at school, for example, and see it as a place they enjoyed coming to:

> I would hope that the children would come in and go home happy from school... I think getting good co-operation from the children is more important than the academics and that a child who is shy comes out of him or herself and that a child who is weak improves and you can see them gelling together as a group (grade 2 teacher, Churchfield)

> My immediate goals are to teach the children the necessities of the curriculum like English and maths but overall I'd like them to turn out happy well rounded children... to be able to turn their hand to anything, not to be uncomfortable in any situation, not feel inhibited or self-conscious (grade 5 teacher, Hillview)

Observational data identified aspects of teacher practice that indicated some pursuit of these goals. But a range of other values, implicit and explicit, were also evident. These can be categorised into three distinct yet interrelated areas: self, interaction with others and work.

Values related to self

Throughout the school day, children were required to monitor and control their behaviour in line with school norms – many of which centred around personal habits, related to time-keeping, dress, diet, as well as behavioural habits, related to self-control such as fidgeting, being patient, not shouting out, taking turns and taking responsibility for one's own actions:

> 'If you've got something to say you must put up your hand'
> 'Who's that being silly?... David! At your age. No, sorry, we can't all talk together'
> 'I'm going round to give stars to children who are in full uniform'
> 'It's not my responsibility if you can't find your copy... go and take a sheet until you find it yourself'

The promotion of a positive sense of self was evident throughout the day, in the form of frequent praise given to children when they completed work, demonstrated kindness to others or when they engaged in behaviour which the teacher approved of .

'There are excellent workers in this class'
'You're a great girl'
'That's brilliant'

Values related to interaction with others

The control of self required in school mirrors the control that is expected in interacting with others. The values explicitly promoted, especially with younger children, were about telling the truth, not disturbing others, showing respect to adults and to one another and responding immediately to the teachers' requests.

'It's interesting to see the children who can do what they are told immediately'
'That's no way to talk to the teacher'
'Say you are sorry and make friends'
'You were excellent. That's the way I expect you to behave when a visitor comes into the class'

Values related to work

The control of self and laying a foundation for positive interaction are part and parcel of the preparation of children for the business of work in school. The associated values are about furnishing children with the self-discipline required for school learning to take place. Teachers' interaction with children, however, was almost exclusively work oriented and accordingly the values related to promoting a positive work ethic predominated. Children were constantly reminded that their work should be neat and tidy, finished quickly and correctly without wasting time and, above all, that they should make their best effort.

'A sign for me that everyone has done their best is that they have written a whole page'
'Don't take all day about doing that exercise'
'Everyone should be on at least question four by now'
'You shouldn't have to think about this for too long'

> 'Do as many as you can, as neatly as you can and do your best'
>
> 'Now we'll see how good your memories are; thinking, looking, listening, concentrating, I want to see signs of that'

The notion of children's work as 'private property' was frequently endorsed and children who copied or worked together were admonished:

> 'Are you telling Shane the answers John? Tut! Tut!'
>
> 'Children you must work on your own'
>
> 'Right hands down, write your own work. I don't want you to have the same as your neighbour'

Although teachers appeared very focused and matter of fact in their pedagogical style, interview data highlighted a more ambiguous and self-critical side. Teachers spoke of how they had changed or adapted their goals with experience, for example, having become more sensitive to the negotiated context of teaching and learning:

> I've changed an awful lot... I suppose when I started I would have taught pretty much the way I was taught and expect every single child to be listening, pencils down and dare any of them take their pencils up... but that was a way of keeping the lid on them... but now I've got the idea of ignoring the negative... I find it's easier to cope and you focus more on the positive... when you have a difficult class you have to change your style... there's less conflict and the children are happier which is better in the long run (grade 5 teacher, Parkway)

> I know I can be very strict and I think especially with the younger children you have to come down to their level a little bit... and I think I have mellowed... I've learned that from the children and watching other teachers in action and how children can work with them or against them (grade 2 teacher, Churchfield)

Concluding remarks

This chapter has focused primarily on pedagogical practice: how the teachers structured the learning environment for their pupils. It looked at how classroom space was organised, and at the climate of interaction between teachers and pupils as they went about the business of teaching and learning. Central to our analyses is the manner in which such practices communicate certain values related to learning, education and childhood. Teacher priorities for children's learning was reflected in the deliberate structuring of classroom space to provide a pleasant, secure and stimulating environment for pupils, but also one where their behaviour was easily monitored and controlled. The public display of children's work, the seating arrangements of the children and the positioning of the teachers' desk were all informed by views as to what schooling and education was all about. Through their pedagogical practices, the teachers structured childhood as a period of socialisation, prioritising norms related to self-discipline, social responsibility and working hard. Their constructions of children that they based predominantly on ability and attentiveness also informed their pedagogical strategies, and so did the pupils' social class background. The greater focus on discipline and control in Parkway was apparent in the formal arrangement of the desks in rows (limiting children's potential for interaction with one another) while in more middle class Churchfield, children were seated in groups.

Disciplinary strategies were employed in every classroom. Discipline was generally viewed in positive terms, facilitating the creation of a learning environment which was ordered and secure for the children. Issues of the children's autonomy rarely emerged in the teachers' talk, suggesting that this was not a priority or focus of their pedagogical practice. Indeed the order and stability operating in their classrooms, coupled with teachers' capacity to frame children's learning in specific ways, is testament to their power in their relations with their pupils. Where such control was not guaranteed, as in the case of Parkway, a complex system of rewards and punishments was employed in an attempt to normalise pupil behaviour in line with teacher goals. The reliance on extrinsic motivation rather than, for example, radical changes in structuring these students' learning experiences points to a tendency to utilise discipline for the purposes of containment and social control rather than necessarily for learning and self empowerment[5]. Overall, the analysis reveals the highly contained nature of classroom life, in which the teachers' behaviour is predominantly geared toward the management of children in time and space through a variety of strategies for discipline and control. This is a central aspect of the exercise of power in schools.

Its impact will be better understood when we look at the children's perspectives on classroom pedagogy. This is the subject of Chapter 5.

Notes

1   The teachers comments here indicate how they classify children according to their values and priorities in education. Thus children are defined as 'chatty', 'bright', 'weak' ,'quiet' signaling an emphasis in particular on ability and behaviour in how the teachers classify children. In Chapter 6 we see how children internalise these classifications into their own constructions of themselves as pupils in school.

2   Teachers frequently intermingled Irish and English phrases in their instructions: 'ag obair' translates as 'working'. Such intermingling adds a certain formality to the tone of the instruction.

3   The use of such reward systems is a good example of what Giddens refers to as the 'dialectic of control', where all relations centred on power involve the negotiation of behaviour to achieve certain outcomes. This is dealt with more fully in Chapter 7. In this instance the reward points are an important negotiating device to ensure at least some compliance by these children to the norms and values of the school.

4   The analysis here owes much to the work of Pollard (1985 and 1987).

5   What is at issue here is the socially reproductive nature of education, where social class positions are reproduced rather than eliminated through the practices teachers engage in in school. For further discussion see for example Anyon, 1981; Bourdieu and Passeron, 1977; Lynch, 1989; MacRuairc, 1997.

5

Children's Perspectives on Pedagogical Practice

Introduction

The previous chapter set the context for examining children's perspectives on the manner in which their time and space is organised in school. Other research in this area, which is limited, focuses on children's assumptions regarding the natural authority of teachers, the absence of their autonomy in school activities and how issues of discipline and control are a major concern in young people's experience of school (Bodine, 2003; Cullingford, 1991; Goodnow and Burns, 1991; Leach and Moon, 1999; Lynch and Lodge, 2002; Pollard and Triggs, 2000). This chapter presents data related to children's perspectives on the pedagogical practices in their schools. It presents their views on the control of their activity in time and space, on discipline procedures and their perspectives on teaching style and practice.

The control of children's time and space in school

Children's views were sought on the organisation and control of their time and space in school. In relation to the organisation of their time, 38% expressed the view that teachers controlled their activity all the time, while a further 40% stated that teachers controlled their activities some of the time. Such control is explicit in the comment of one child, to the general agreement of her peers, that being in school was a bit like being a robot:

> Sometimes it feels like a bit like being a robot... like as if the teacher is in the middle of the room with a great big remote control and you have to do everything she says or you will get into trouble (grade 2 girl, Churchfield)

That the children find this control acceptable is reflected in the responses of 64% of the sample, who stated that it was 'okay' for teachers to exercise control over what they did in school. Such acceptance appeared to be influenced by gender and age, with girls and younger children most acquiescent:

> I think the teacher should choose cos then there would be no arguments... some of the class likes some things that half the class doesn't (grade 5 girl, Parkway)

> The teachers don't really let you do what you want... so they don't give much power to the children... the teachers have the most power and make the children learn what they want them to learn (grade 5 boy, Churchfield)

Children were frustrated with the lack of choice or consultation afforded them. This centred on the working of the timetable and the children's perception that this reflected teacher priorities and values, described in Chapter 3. The majority of children in the study (79%) were favourably disposed toward the manner in which their space was organised in school and felt that it was the teachers' responsibility to decide how this should be done. Favourable comments were made about teachers' efforts to decorate the classrooms with children's work:

> I think our classroom looks brilliant... cos of all the art work an the spiders hangin down from the ceilin... there's lots of things hangin down... I feel when I walk into the classroom in the mornin that it's like fairy land... it's sort of weird (grade 2 boy, Parkway)

During the interviews children expressed the view that teachers are, in essence, being paid to direct them in terms both of their time and organisation of space in school and that this is necessary if children are to learn and do well in their exams[1]. They often express this in terms of the teacher bossing the children – that to be a teacher is to be paid for 'bossing' them:

> The teachers have the most power cos they are able to tell the children what to do and if the children don't do it they get into trouble... I would like to be a teacher cos when you are doing art you would be the first to try it out and you get to boss everybody around and tell them they are not so clever (grade 2 girl, Churchfield)

> The teachers... they're grown ups so they're meant to be the bosses (grade 5 boy, Parkway)

Some differences in the children's responses to these questions were associated with ability, gender and age level. Children who perceived themselves to be of weaker ability, for example, were more negative about teacher control over their space (P<.001). This undoubtedly relates to the tendency for teachers to place such children closer to their desks so they can be easily monitored. Boys and older children were also more likely to express negative views about the control of their space (P<.001) – again related to the tendency for teachers to spend more time monitoring their behaviour by means of the seating arrangements.

Further insights into the children's perception of the control and organisation of their space in school emerged in the interviews. Two specific themes emerged: space as a form of symbolic power between teachers and pupils, and the importance of child culture in children's experience of space in school.

Space as a form of symbolic power

The distribution of power between teachers and children is reflected in the use and allocation of space in the school, what Foucault (1979) refers to as the 'architectural composition of space'. There are for example clearly defined adult and child zones in schools and while adults can move freely in and out of any of these zones, children can not. As relatively forbidden spaces, these adult zones (e.g staffroom, principal's office) can consequently evoke a sense of awe in children, and this may be reinforced for example by a teacher threatening to send a misbehaving child to the principal's office.

Similar issues arise in relation to the ownership of the school/ classroom space itself and how such ownership both reflects and increases the teachers' power within the school. When the children were asked to express their opinion on who the school 'belonged to', 54% said the principal, 7% the teachers and 27 % said that the local council owned the school. Only 2% of children expressed the view that the school belonged to them. Justifications by the children for the greater authority exercised by teachers were linked to this issue of ownership – if the principal/teachers own the school, then they are entitled to do what they want with it and within it:

> The principal and the teacher decides the rules... cos they own the school (grade 5 girls, Parkway)

> It's her classroom so she can do it whatever way she wants (grade 5 girl, Churchfield)

Within the schools teachers had access to the staffroom, where they could relax and eat hot food and which was mostly out of bounds for the children. The existence of the staffroom and the absence of a similar facility for children is an important symbolic space within the school in terms of the exercise of power:

> In the staffroom they have really cushy seats and a cooker and a microwave... I don't like going into it cos you have all the teachers there looking at you (grade 5 boy, Hillview)

> I think we should have a little room, like a cafeteria... the teachers can go in and out of the staffroom if they want or in and out of the yard... teachers can decide what they want and when and where they want it (grade 5 girl, Churchfield)

The space within the school set aside specifically for children is the schoolyard. The relatively barren appearance of this space in all three of the schools visited itself indicates the lower status of children in the school hierarchy. While all children value their 'yard' time, they are critical of the lack of both space and facilities available to them during their break:

> I wouldn't call it a playground cos there is nothing to do except run around (grade 5 boy, Hillview)

> It would be good if there were swings and slides and things in the yard (grade 5 girl, Churchfield)

The furniture the children and teachers have access to also symbolically reflects the differential power between the two groups[2]:

> It would be good if there were cushions for the chairs... teachers have big comfortable chairs and they have drawers in their desks and they don't have to share a desk... we have about that much space between two people (grade 5 boy, Church field)

> I wish we had more comfortable chairs... the teachers have them because they are grown ups... they don't respect children... teachers are respected more by the principal and other teachers (grade 5, Churchfield)

The fact that the children perceive the teachers' furniture as being more comfortable demonstrates the status differential between themselves and adults in the school. However the lack of comfort of the children's furniture also conveys to them the value that is being placed on work and concentration over comfort and relaxation:

> The teachers have big deadly chairs... they can just sit back (grade 5 boy, Parkway)

> If we get too comfortable on the chair we'd probably doze off or something... or not work that well (grade 5 girl, Churchfield)

Control of children's behaviour is also exercised through the physical layout of furniture in the classroom. Children's views on how their seating should be arranged differs according to how much they wish to engage in 'back-stage' behaviour (Giddens, 1987). Of concern here is the avoidance of being caught chatting with friends or doing homework during school hours:

> I'd put the teacher's desk as far away as possible... outside the classroom door... cos she's watching your every move... every time you even look in your bag she's watching over you... and if you want to get a headstart in your homework... she sees you... she's really stern like that and sometimes she walks all around the place and when she's coming over you hear a big shuffle (grade 5 girl, Hillview)

> I don't like the classroom cos sometimes the teacher moves us an I'm always stuck up at the front of her desk (grade 5 girl, Hillview)

Such comments confirm the children's awareness of being watched and monitored by teachers, a goal teachers deliberately pursued in the organisation of seating arrangements as we have seen.

Child culture and the control of children's space in school

Teasing is a central feature of child interaction at school. While many children, for example, commented favourably on the decor in their classrooms, particularly the brightness resulting from the display of art work, some expressed wariness about their own paintings being put on public view lest they were teased about them by their peers:

> I'd prefer if she didn't put our paintings up on the wall or at least that we could decide... cos if you did something useless you get slagged for it (grade 5 boy, Churchfield).

The fear of being teased, as well as the desire to have fun and cope with the uncertainties that are part and parcel of classroom life, makes children want to be in the company of their friends. This desire is evident in their comments about seating arrangements:

> She doesn't know what it's like to be us... like we can't see our friends and not talk to them... it's like seeing someone in the street and not talking to them... we should be able to pick who we sit beside (grade 5 girl, Churchfield)

However, children also want some measure of privacy in the crowded atmosphere of the classroom and some said they wanted to to be separate from others and to have a dedicated space to put things in:

> I'd prefer if we were sitting in rows... you have more privacy and no-one can look into your copy... you can block them off with your book (grade 5 boy, Hillview)

> Lockers would be a good idea cos at least you'd have somewhere to put your stuff and it wouldn't get robbed or all dirty... and you'd have your privacy cos all the boys push our books onto the floor (grade 5 girl, Parkway)

Within child culture, gender is an important determinant of social interaction. Single sex friendship groups are the norm. The interview data suggests, however, that children perceive that teachers use gender as a disciplinary mechanism, to reduce inattentiveness in the class and specifically to encourage boys to work harder:

> I think it should be boy girl boy girl cos then if a boy is with a girl... boys hate girls so they won't talk at all... their writing would come all neat as well cos they wouldn't be messing (grade 5 girl, Hillview)

> It used to be the girls together and the boys together and if you were bold you used to have to sit with the girls for ten minutes (grade 5 boy, Parkway)

Such comments indicate that these children perceive girls to be the bearers of adult norms, responsible for encouraging more positive behaviour in boys through their example. The similarity in attitudes to those expressed by teachers in the study (Chapter 2) is significant and suggests that children have internalised dominant teacher perceptions of gender differences, into their self-perceptions. Decisions made by teachers relating to the seating of children by gender sharply highlight how intrinsic the organisation of space is to the exercise of power in schools. In this instance it serves to normalise the behaviour of boys while confirming the perception of girls as the bearers of social responsibility.[3]

Discipline and the exercise of power

The control of children's time and space in school takes place within a disciplinary framework in which they are required to monitor their behaviour in line with the rules and regulations. Conformity to these rules is part of the process of socialisation and is tied to the power dynamic between adults and children. The type of rules formulated, who decides them, to whom they apply and the reasons for their existence reflect not only the values and norms which are considered important in society but also the exercise of power between adults and children in schools. Observational data confirmed that values related to self (self-control, diet, dress) were implicit in teachers' pedagogical practice, as were values about work (neat, correct, private property) and interaction with others (respect, telling the truth).

I asked the children questions relating to school rules. I wanted to know about their attitudes to and perceptions of the rules they follow in school and, by implication, the discourses/constructions of childhood they drew on when expressing these views.

Children's perception of school rules

Children were asked to specify the rules they followed in class. Table 5.1 below indicates the frequency of the rules mentioned, and the spontaneous responses of the children are coded for analysis into these categories:

Table 5.1: Children's perception of the rules they must follow in school

Rules which I must follow	N	%
Rules re: how I can move about	51	38.3
Rules re: what I can say	29	21.8
Rules re: what I wear	1	0.8
Rules re: what I can eat	11	8.3
Rules re: paying attention	13	9.8
Rules re: how I mix with others	18	13.5
No Answer	10	7.5
Totals	133	100.0

The table indicates that rules relating to the control of movement (running, being out of place, going to the toilet) speech (shouting, cursing) and social interaction (fighting, politeness, bullying, being cheeky, spitting) are foremost in children's minds. Subsequent analysis of second and third mentions confirmed this pattern. Class level was shown to be significantly associated ($p<.001$) with the frequency a rule is mentioned, with younger children more conscious of the need to be attentive and older children more likely to focus on rules related to the control of their movement. Gender was also a factor: boys were more inclined to focus on the control of their speech while girls emphasised rules related to their level of attentiveness ($P<.001$). Social class was also found to be significant: the children in working class Parkway were more sensitive to rules related to their manner of speech and movement, whereas the middle class children were more likely to mention rules related to their general attentiveness. ($P<.0001$). Girls, middle class children and younger children appeared to be tuned into issues related to work and attentiveness, while boys, working class children and older children were most conscious of rules which constrained their verbal expression and physical movement.

Examples of rules within each category are evident in the children's comments:

> No running, no talking, playing nicely, listening (grade 2 boy, Churchfield)

> No eating, no cursing, no fighting, no answering back (grade 5 girl, Parkway)

When asked to state their perception of the reasons for school rules, a majority of children expressed the view that rules were there for 'self-control' and protection. Boys and middle class children were most likely to mention the latter. Comments during interviews reflect these patterns:

> They have rules so children won't hurt themselves and to teach them discipline... cos if you learn discipline the older you get the wiser you become (grade 5 girl, Churchfield)

> Sometimes the rules are good and sometimes they are not... like if you do something and your not proud of it an you think: 'God, them rules are good' cos you feel proud when you follow them... if you done something bold that your not allowed do you might say: 'oh God I hate them rules'... like say someone lost a bit of jewellery and you found it you'd give it back to them... then you'd be proud of yourself... but your not allowed have tattoos... I wish you were (grade 2 boy, Parkway)

The children's perceptions of whether or not school rules are fair revealed a certain ambiguity among the sample, with 37.6% stating they were sometimes fair and 34% that they were fair. Children from a working class background were more inclined to agree that rules were fair, as were younger children ($P<.001$ and $P<.0001$ respectively). The rules perceived as being fair mainly related to making school safe and tended to draw on a discourse that perceived of children as being wild and in need of containment:

> If there wasn't school rules then children would end up in hospital (grade 5 girl, Hillview)

> There are rules in school cos children are bad (grade 2 girl, Parkway)

> If we didn't have rules we'd be battering the teachers around... we'd only be having fun (grade 5 boy, Parkway)

Such comments demonstrate a discourse that defines children in terms of dependence and as needing adult protection and guidance. The data also suggests that where children held ambiguous or negative views of school rules, it was mainly because these interfered with their desire to have fun. These dichotomies in response are reflected in the interview data. We see two competing discourses influencing the children's comments – one which views children in a paternalistic fashion and one which seeks to challenge this:

> They have rules so children won't hurt themselves and to teach them discipline... cos if you learn discipline the older you get the wiser you become (grade 5 boy, Hillview)

> It is right for grown ups to decide for children cos they have the best interest for us... or else we would be swinging out of the rafters all the time (grade 5 girl, Parkway)

> School rules aren't fair cos we should be allowed have fun sometimes... rules do make school safer but they make it too safe... they shouldn't really stop you from running or eating what you want (grade 5 boy, Churchfield)

Children's views about the fairness or otherwise of rules was also affected by the inconsistency among teachers in establishing and implementing the rules. This can confuse children about the behaviour required of them:

> The walking around rule and the talking rule is usually the same for all teachers but sometimes other teachers would have rules about being allowed to whisper and then another teacher would say: 'oh you are allowed to whisper' and then another teacher would say: 'Oh you are not allowed to whisper or talk or anything, you just have to be quiet and listen' (grade 5 girl, Hillview)

> Last year our teacher told us always in our maths copies we have to do four lines... two along the side and two in the middle and then you'd start writing... but this year the teacher says we need only do one line in the middle... it is confusing cos you have to get used to doing it and then once we get used to it we go into a different class and then we have to get used to a different set of rules (grade 5 boy, Churchfield)

These comments indicate how children seek to ascertain the rule frames (Davies, 1982; Pollard and Triggs, 2000) by which teachers operate and how confused they are when rule frames change. It also demonstrates the manner in which issues related to rules and rule following frequently reflect individual teacher ideologies as much as general perceptions about what are considered appropriate norms for children's behaviour in schools.

That teachers exercise almost complete control over decisions related to school rules is evident from the 86% of the sample who stated that the teacher decides what the rules will be. While a majority agreed with this trend, their responses, at 52%, were slightly more conditional than the agreement expressed over the teacher deciding how their classroom space should be organised and how they should spend their time (see page 68). Again, girls and younger children were generally more accepting of teacher authority in this respect, justifying the level of teacher control by asserting that rules helped learning, kept children safe and were the domain of the teacher as 'she should be in charge'. Conversely boys and older children, especially those who were middle class, tended to argue for children's right to a voice in the making of school rules and that school rules were hard to keep. Comments during the interviews highlighted the dichotomy in children's views between those who fully supported teacher authority in these matters, and those who questioned the level of teacher control:

> The teacher decides the rules... that's fair cos if the children were allowed they'd be saying we're allowed run around the classroom... and all the parents would be taking all the children out of the school cos they wouldn't learn anything (grade 5 girl,

> It would be better to share decisions with children... at the start of the year he just comes in with a long list and says now abide by the rules... and that's not fair... it's like boarding school but we're here in an ordinary school (grade 5 boy, Parkway)

These comments reflect the competing discourses on children and childhood that influence the perspectives held in schools – one that perceives children as incapable of acting responsibly, with the implication that they should not be taken seriously, and a second discourse that seeks to have children's voices heard in school. The following excerpt from an interview with a group of grade 5 girls in Parkway illustrates the contrasting discourses:

> *Lorna*: The pupils have the least power cos they don't have nice things and they can't do anything they want... I think there should be children's meetings as well... a student council like on the telly... and have votes and all

> *Louise*: but no one would take it seriously... cos the kids would all start messing and laughing... all the boys and all... I think the teachers would take it seriously but we couldn't go on strike or anything even though they go on strike... they would just say: 'get in here now'... you'd get lines and all'

The positioning of teachers in terms of authority and control and the negative impact on children's construction of themselves as power holders within the school is also evident in the children's attitudes toward the level of control exercised over teacher behaviour. Where children identified restrictions in teachers' capacity for action (and this was held most ambiguously by younger children), this tended to centre on an awareness of teachers not being allowed to hit or abuse children, and having to act in a socially responsible manner:

> The teachers must be a good influence on the children and they must try and give them a good education and they must be strict (grade 5 boy, Churchfield)

> The only rules I know the teachers are not allowed break is cursing at the children or hitting them but the principal broke it (grade 5 girl, Parkway).

For the most part, however, children viewed teachers as having great freedom within the school[4] characterised by their capacity to move about freely, talk whenever they want and eat whatever they want:

> The teachers can leave the classroom whenever they like... she gives us a few sentences to write and then she would come back in and she would say: 'God! did I not give you work to do' (grade 5 girl, Hillview)

> The teachers are allowed smoke... they're allowed walk around the classroom whenever they want... they're allowed talk whenever they want... they're allowed have cups of tea in the middle of school when we are doing our work... and that's not fair cos we are not allowed even have a sandwhich... and if

they don't bring in lunch they can send someone across to the shop (grade 5, boy, Parkway)

The negotiated context of school discipline

Despite the children's perception of both the autonomy and greater power of the teachers, such control was by no means complete. While these children seek some level of consultation over the establishment of school rules, teachers' awareness of the tenuous and negotiated character of learning is evident from the range of strategies they employ to ensure compliance with school norms. For example, observational data highlighted the complex system of stars and points used in Parkway to encourage some level of discipline and this gave rise to mixed responses among the children themselves over the use of such systems[5]:

> I think the points are stupid... we had a rule last your that if you fell below 5 points you get suspended... well one boy is at four points now and he's not suspended (grade 5 boy, Parkway)

> I think the points are good but Miss goes easy on the bold people cos if we do something bold she goes really hard on us cos she knows we can do our best if we're good... but the bold people never do their best hardly and Miss knows that and she lets them carry on (grade 5 girl, Parkway).

Playing on children's desire for fun, teachers also seek to maintain control by setting one subject off against another – trying to create the balance children seek between work time and playtime. Reduced homework or the threat of extra homework, the promise of doing or not doing Art and Physical Education, watching a video, are all used as means of encouraging conformity and learning. In spite of the teachers' efforts, however, the children's talk was suffused with the control the teachers exerted and made little acknowledgement that this was something the teachers strove for, often under challenging circumstances. The children saw teacher control as relatively complete, maintained through varied systems of surveillance, which were often interpreted in terms of 'magical' powers of detection:

> The teachers on yard duty have a notebook and if your name goes in it twice you are in deep trouble (grade 5 girl, Churchfield)

> She makes you kind of nervous... you're afraid even to whisper to your neighbour beside you... it's like she knows you are going to talk... she's right beside you... it's like she has a sense that she knows... it's like magic (grade 5 girl, Hillview)

> I do think the teacher has eyes in the back of her head cos when she's out of the room she knows stuff that happened and even if she's sitting at her desk she is looking at the side of her eye to see who is even whispering (grade 2 girl, Churchfield)

The comments reveal the children's sense that they are under constant surveillance and must adjust their behaviour accordingly. As experienced by one child in Hillview:

> She never lets anything pass... she always has to be in control of everything... she has to know what every single person in the class is doing... what they are saying to each other... what everybody is writing to each other... she's kind of a control freak... you can hardly take a breadth of fresh air (grade 5 girl)

Child culture and children's experience of school rules

During the interviews on school rules, issues emerged that indicate the influence of child culture on children's perspectives and attitudes toward the rules they must follow in school. Much of the analysis to date has indicated that some children, specifically girls and younger children, have a more positive disposition than boys and older children to school rules and emphasise the safety aspect of rules. Understanding the dynamics of child culture in terms of how boys and girls interact and how younger and older children interact helps to explain the differences identified:

> If we didn't have rules then everything would be messy and the big children would go down where the infants are... and the big boys and girls would knock them down (grade 2 girl, Churchfield)

> Children don't obey rules cos they're fighting and that... even though that's a real boys thing that is... some girls are rough... I'm real rough cos I stand up for myself... I just punch the fellas around... knock them on the ground... so the boys can't push me around... if you don't hit them back they'll bully you. (grade 5 girl, Parkway)

Because adults in the school have greater authority, children expect them to intervene to protect them when disputes get out of hand and are annoyed when their pleas to do so are ignored:

> A boy came over to me the other day and hit me and I said get lost or I'll dig your head in and I went over to the teacher and told him and then he goes: 'Okay... I'll go and sort that out now' and he's just standing there like that and I go over and ask him again did he sort it out an he says: 'no' and says he'll do some-thind about it later and he doesn't (grade 5 boys, Parkway)

While children may subscribe to the 'no fighting rule' when they are under attack, the reasons they put forward as to why some children do not follow school rules reveal further important features of child culture:

Table 5.2: Reasons why children do not follow school rules

Reasons children do not follow rules:	N	%
Want to be cool/popular	17	12.8
Don't like them	37	27.8
The rules are unfair	20	15.0
The rules are hard to follow	5	3.8
To get attention	5	3.8
The children are bold	23	17.3
No Answer	26	19.5
Totals	133	100.0

The table highlights certain features of child culture: disobeying rules in an effort to be cool (12.8%), not liking the restrictive nature of rules (27.8%) and perceiving rules to be unfair (15.0%). Cross tabulations indicated significant differences related to class level ($P<.001$) with younger children internalising the adult voice and most inclined to stress the 'boldness' of children who do not follow rules (17.3%).

The interview data highlights the tension created for the older children who subscribe to the norms of child culture which emphasises having fun in school and not being seen to work too hard. Such traits in turn are deemed to improve one's status within the peer group:

> Sometimes children don't follow rules cos they have to... or else their friends will say: 'oh you never get into trouble you

are a really goody goody, you're a little lick to the teacher' (grade 5 girl, Hillview)

I'd love to have the brains and the knowledge but you wouldn't want to be a loner with no friends or anything... if Mick was a loner we'd bring him back in and make him popular by not letting him get too much into his work... cos then people would call him a swot (grade 5 boy, Churchfield)

The data also indicates that children have a perception of what it is to be a child and part of that perception is doing things adults have forbidden them to do. Fighting, running, shouting, having fun are part of what it is to be a child and following adult defined rules is often perceived to interfere with this:

A lot of children run and chase in the yard... it's the only way to have fun... you can't just stand around (grade 5 boy, Church-field)

Everybody has to break the no running rule at least one time... I don't know... it's just the way children are... we play chasing and we run... (*to the researcher: don't tell the teachers*)... everybody has to break a rule in their life... we don't want to break the rule but we just want to do the activity (grade 5 girl, Churchfield)

Some children actively resist teacher control by making the teacher angrier and angrier:

Punishment makes you even more angry and you'll do things even more to annoy the teacher (grade 5 boy, Churchfield)

I was chewing something all morning and you're not allowed to eat in class. I was messing and the teacher gave me lines: 'I must not chew in class', and I did them: 'I must chew in class'. I forgot to put the 'not' in and she was really angry and her face was as red as an apple and she started yelling at everyone and looking at me all the time (grade 5 boy, Parkway)

These attempts to undermine teacher control and authority indicate that such children understand that teachers are not as powerful as they may at first seem. Others use more discreet tactics:

I brought popcorn in and she took it off me... and some people just told me to faint so then the teacher would say: 'oh sorry

> here's your popcorn... I'll give you more sweets tomorrow'...
> cos they wouldn't want you to tell your parents that you had no
> lunch if that's all you brought in for lunch (grade 5 girl, Church-
> field)

Many rules are abandoned or defied when children are free from the watchful eyes of teachers... such as in the toilets, corridors or during break time:

> You just do what you can do and if you can't you can't... but we
> don't really follow the rules in the yard or in the corridor... we
> have races in the corridor (grade 5 girl, Churchfield)

An examination of child culture reveals many of the tensions and contradictions that arise for children over their experience and attitudes toward school rules. While being a child means doing things which adults don't always agree with (fighting, running wild, having fun), each individual child must also negotiate a path between adult/peer approval. Fear of being slagged for over adherence to school rules must be set against fear of rebuke from adults for not getting work done. Both teachers and children use a variety of strategies to accommodate to these competing pressures, highlighting the negotiated character of classroom life and the fact that absolute control is never guaranteed. That girls and young children are positively disposed to the safety aspect of rules and boys and older children most negatively disposed to teacher control over them, reflects the dynamics of approval and status enhancement within their peer groups.

How children perceive teaching style and practice

The way children are organised for learning and the manner in which they are taught is an important part of pedagogical practice in schools and affects not only their self-esteem and ability concepts but also the friendship groups they enter into (Devine, 1991; Oakes 1985; Pollard and Triggs, 2000; Smyth, 1999). Highlighting children's preference for class teaching styles as well as their perception of what makes a good teacher pinpoints the ways children experience the learning environment and what motivates them to learn.

Children were asked what method of teaching they preferred. Just under 50% expressed a preference for whole class teaching, while

30% said they liked to be taught in groups. The reasons they gave (spontaneously) for their preferences focused on better learning (32%), privacy (14%), speed of getting through work (10%) or a desire for all children to be treated in the same way (13%). Whole class teaching was chosen by pupils primarily because of the desire for all of them to be treated the same, whereas individual and group methods were chosen for reasons of privacy and improved learning. Comments during interviews reflect the tension within child culture in terms of the avoidance of being seen to be learning because such exposure puts them at risk of being teased by peers. Furthermore they wish to avoid being overly visible to the teacher so that they can have support from their peers if they want it.

> I prefer working on my own cos if you get something wrong and everybody laughs... that won't happen... you have the teacher there beside you if you get stuck and she learns you better (grade 5 boy, Parkway)

> I prefer small groups cos if you are stuck on something you can tap the other person on the shoulder and they will help you... if you're on your own you won't have any help (grade 5 girl, Hillview)

Children's views on levels of satisfaction with how they were taught were evenly divided between those who were happy and those who would like teaching to be done differently. Older children were more likely to be critical of the manner in which they were taught (P<.01) and to give reasons that related to work pressures and the imbalance between work and fun activities as detailed in Chapter 2:

> I wouldn't be as hard as they are because I'd know how it feels (grade 5 girl, Parkway)

> I'd make learning more fun and stop all the rules... and I'd have work followed by football and give the children an hour where they could decide what to do (grade 5 boy, Churchfield)

A more indepth understanding of the children's expectations regarding teaching is evident from their views as to what makes a 'good' teacher.

Children's notions of a good teacher

When asked to specify what made a good teacher, the children's responses could be categorised into four main areas related to: personal trait's/characteristics (intelligent, physical trait's), teaching skills, social interaction with children (polite, kind, happy, patient) and the use of discipline\exertion of power over children (strict, fair). The frequency of responses in each category is recorded in Table 5.3 below:

Table 5.3 Children's perception of what makes a good teacher

What makes a good teacher:	N	%
Personal Traits	8	6.0
Teaching Skills	37	27.8
Manner of Interaction with Children	56	42.2
Discipline/Power over Children	10	7.5
No Answer	22	16.5
Totals	133	100.0

As noted in chapter 2, younger children were more likely to stress how teachers interacted with them (being nice/kind etc.) whereas older children emphasised issues related to the teacher's exercise of discipline and power as well as how she interacted with them. Gender differences were also identified (P<.05): girls were more sensitive to how teachers interacted with them, while boys focused to a greater extent on teaching skills and the teachers' personal traits. Qualities that teachers brought to bear in their teaching were also emphasised by grade 5 children, for example whether the teacher was patient and explained things clearly to them:

In maths she might explain something by doing two sums and if you didn't understand them then tough... she'll say: 'I'm not taking any questions after this... so you better all listen' and even if you did listen and you tried to understand it and you couldn't she wouldn't answer you... she has no patience (grade 5 girl, Churchfield)

I hate the way if you don't understand something and you say you don't... the teacher just explains it the same way all over again... they don't change the way they explain so you still don't understand' (grade 5 boy, Hillview)

The comments suggest that children do want to understand what they are taught but that some perceive their teachers as lacking in patience, time and skill to give them the individual attention they require to learn effectively. It was also clear during the interviews that a tension exists for older children between the definition of the teacher as one who teaches in a fun/interesting manner and allows children greater freedom, but who is also strict and ensures adequate learning. The ideal teacher is perceived to be one who gets the balance right, satisfying children's immediate needs for interest and fun while at the same time fulfilling long terms needs of learning and achievement in school:

> The teacher we had last year wasn't so strict... he didn't really control the class... he allowed children talk more... it was good for us but my mam didn't like it... she thought we weren't getting any work done... we were just messing and he wasn't strict enough... he did a little less work maybe than our teacher does now but we still got the basics and he'd let you take a drink of water if you were thirsty and that (grade 5 girl, Churchfield)

> Sometimes be nice and sometimes be strict... you can't be nice all the time cos children will break the rules... a bad teacher is if they are nice all the time and don't give the children any discipline (grade 5 girl, Hillview)

Further definitions of what makes a good teacher emerge in the comparisons drawn by one class of children between a student teacher and the 'real' teacher. They deemed the 'real' teacher to have qualities they appreciated, to do with organisation, discipline, teaching skill and an understanding of children because of her teaching experience:

> Sometimes the student teacher goes on and on and on and takes ages to get organised... like twenty minutes was wasted in PE getting ready... the teachers have more experience (grade 5 girl, Hillview)

> The student teacher doesn't know the messers in the class... and they don't understand the pupils as much cos they are younger... when the teachers have children of their own they understand kids better (grade 5 boy, Hillview)

Concluding comments

A consideration of children's experience of pedagogical practice highlights the level of control they perceive to exist over the organisation of their time and space in school. While this was evident in the rules and regulations which they are required to follow, other factors such as seating arrangements and the restricted access to certain spaces in school also conveyed the almost taken for granted surveillance that is part and parcel of their school experience. Their attitudes toward such control appear to be predicated mainly on their understanding of what school is about and what the teachers' role should be. In this sense children are clear that the teachers' role is one of authority and that they are essentially being paid to 'boss' the children and tell them what to do. Their views in many ways parallel those of the teachers, outlined in Chapter 4. They perceive that control is both inevitable and necessary to satisfy the long-term goals of learning and education and to create a safe environment in which such learning can take place.

However the children's views also suggest disconnectedness from the space of school itself, symbolised by their assumption that the school belongs to adults rather than children and consequently reflects adult-defined priorities and goals in its practice. While children were generally appreciative of their teachers' efforts to make their classrooms attractive spaces, their negative views (for example about seating arrangements, rules about talking) focused on how teacher practices interfered with their priority of interacting and having fun with their peers. These findings mirror those related to children's experience of the curriculum as detailed in Chapter 3. Differences were noted between the children in their views however, with boys and older children most critical of the level of control exercised over them, and arguing for the greater involvement of children in decisions about school rules. In their discussions of teaching practices, the children stressed the importance of patience, good explanatory and organisational skills as well as the need to maintain a balance between work and fun in the school day. Criticisms of teacher practice tended to focus on the latter issues, with older children most likely to frame their responses in terms of the continual pressure to work and the absence of any focus on the individual.

In terms of the exercise of power between adults and children, the data reinforces the view of school as a space where children are subjected to a rigorous system of control and regulation over which they have little say. In defining teachers as 'the boss' children implicitly acknowledge this power differential and see it reflected not only in the rules that govern their own behaviour but also in the facilities and resources available to teachers and the teachers' relative freedom to do what they want in school. Given that schooling is compulsory[6], childhood is thus being structured as a period of regulation and confinement in which children must curtail their short-term desire for fun in favour of the longterm benefit of learning. Accordingly, children's talk about school is framed in terms of two competing discourses of childhood, one firmly rooted in the grown up world of work and self-responsibility, the other in the child world of games and freedom from responsibility. Their idea of a good teacher is someone who helps them straddle both worlds – who allows a measure of freedom and fun, while simultaneously imposing enough discipline and regulation for the goals of learning to be realised. For older children, part of the 'freedom' they want involves allowing them to be involved in decisions about the regulation of their school lives, structuring their experience of school in a more democratic manner. That for the most part they are not consulted in this way indicates to them the unfair exercise of power by teachers. Younger children appeared to be satisfied with the control exercised by teachers, interpreting this in a more paternalistic light, as ensuring safety and security in the school environment.

Yet in spite of the level of control exercised over children and their differing perceptions of such control, the data also indicated the parallel world of child culture, where children's desire for fun and games took precedence over rules related to running, shouting and having a laugh. For some children the breaking of adult rules was part of what it meant to be a child and, as noted in Chapter 2, spaces where this could be done (that did not threaten the overall goals of learning) were regularly sought out and exploited. The data also highlighted the intricate power and status matrices in the children's own world and how children could use adult rules for the purpose of protection (from being bullied, for example, or run over by older children in the playground) or for status enhancement (by breaking adult rules), depending on the context involved. Further, attitudes toward teacher practices, such as the public display of school work or using whole class versus grouped teaching methods, were often framed in terms of the knock on effect in their relations with peers, with 'being the same as others' an important criterion in the preferences they expressed. Overall, these patterns reveal the children's management of the control systems in school and their struggle as active agents to interpret, incorporate and accommodate to such systems in terms of their own values and priorities.

Notes

1   This affirms findings detailed in chapter 3 related to children's instrumental orientation to their education.

2   It is also a pertinent example of the use of furniture as part of the 'disciplinary technology' of the school, maximising the body's usefulness to lead to greater learning and concentration. This is discussed in Chapter 7.

3   Similar patterns have been noted in a recent study at second level by Lynch and Lodge (2002).

4   Teachers do not perceive themselves to have such freedom in school and that their own behaviour stems from the demands placed on them to implement the curriculum and satisfy broader societal goals in the education of children. This aspect of teachers' professional lives is considered in greater detail in Chapter 7 and constitutes an important element in the cycle of power in schools and the structural influences on schooling practice.

5   The fact that these children pick up on the inconsistencies in the implementation of the reward points system is testament to the tenuous grasp this teacher has over discipline in the classroom. To stick rigidly to the rules of awarding and taking points away for good/bad behaviour would result in the repeated sanctioning of the 'bold' children, thereby alienating them further. Not to sanction such children however leads to criticisms from those who are compliant, who complain about unfairness or leniency in the discipline system.

6   All children in the Republic of Ireland must receive an education from the age of six to sixteen. While most children receive this education through the formal school system, parents, recognised in the constitution as the primary educators of their children have the right to educate their children at home. A minority do so.

6

The Experience of Evaluation in School

Introduction

Evaluation involves adults in school exercising judgements upon the behaviour and performance of children. It is intrinsic to the exercise of power between adults and children, as decisions related to what is evaluated and even how evaluation is carried out normalise children in terms of dominant values and ideologies. Central among these are values related to ability[1] (what does it mean to be clever?), behaviour (what behaviour is punished and what is rewarded?) and learning (is process or product emphasised?). Evaluation in this sense serves as a connecting thread between curricular and pedagogical practice, as teachers communicate to the children what they should learn and how well they are learning through the appraisal systems they use.

Power is exercised not only in terms of decisions as to what and how evaluation is carried out (thereby influencing for example what is considered as 'real learning', as discussed in Chapter 3) but also through the influence of evaluation on children's own perceptions of what they are 'good' at and 'bad' at in school. The fact that most evaluation in school is carried out in a public and highly visible manner adds to the exercise of this power, as children compare and contrast their performance with that of their peers. Evaluation can be a positive or negative part of children's experience of school, both contributing to and reinforcing children's perception of their academic selves. Other research in this area (e.g. Crocker and Cheesman, 1991; Filer and Pollard, 2000; King, 1989; Pollard and Triggs, 2000; Reay and William, 1999) points to the mixed reactions of children to being assessed in school and how sensitive they are to the judgements their teachers make.

This chapter details findings related to the process of evaluation in the sample schools. The analysis begins by highlighting observational data focusing on the strategies of evaluation adopted by teachers in the study. Attitudes toward the experience of evaluation are then explored, with reference to both children and teacher perspectives. Also explored are the values that are implicit in children's perception of their performance in school. Child culture and its influence on children's experience of being evaluated is also illustrated.

Teacher Strategies for Evaluation

The strategies that teachers adopted in relation to the evaluation of children in their classrooms can be analysed in terms of formal evaluative practices and informal evaluation. Formal evaluation involved assigning tests and correcting exercises, while informal evaluation took place as teachers interacted with children during the course of teaching and learning – praising and/or admonishing them for the work they were doing.

Teachers in all the classes gave children tests[2] in spelling on Fridays. For grade 5, tests were also administered in mathematics and less frequently in subjects such as geography or history. In each instance, the teachers reminded the children that their test work was their 'own'[3] and most children approached the tests in a serious manner. Children were not usually allowed to correct their own work but had to swap with another child in the group. This sometimes caused considerable tension over the accuracy of the corrections made – in red pen:

> Marcus is correcting Mathew's mathematics test. He tells Mathew that he has written 421 for the answer. Mathew replies 'it's 4 you dope'. Marcus seeks confirmation from the teacher who agrees it is a 4 but is written too closely to 21 from the

next sum. She admonishes Mathew for not having bigger spaces between his sums. Marcus returns to his place with a grin on his face. (Field notes, grade 5 Churchfield)

Children's visibility in terms of their ability/performance was heightened not only through such correction practices but also through the public announcement of results – particularly mathematics work and homework:

Any problems with the homework? Hands up all who got their sums right. Everyone's hand should be up. John what happened to you? (Field notes, grade 5 Hillview)

Although children sometimes appeared to be outwardly flippant about poor performance (especially the boys), the threat to self implicit in such public displays of performance was also noteworthy. This is reflected in the comment of one boy in grade 5 in Parkway:

I did shite in those I did. Whoever gets mine (*copy to correct*) don't say how I did cos I did mine stupid.

In the course of correcting work, teachers would frequently advise the whole class on the standard required by basing it on the mistakes one child or several children had made:

While I was correcting the geography work I noticed that Joan and Lorcan did not draw a straight line

'Look! Look! Capital letters for names' (said loudly to a boy whose work the teacher is correcting)

Standards were also enforced by directly comparing one child with another or one group with another:

'This side is excellent. C'mon this side..wake up!'
'In 2/3 minutes the hardest working group will go to the library'
'I can only hear Samantha... the rest of you are half asleep!'

Questioning children orally on the topics they were covering in each curricular area also exposed them in terms of effort and performance. For the younger children such questioning often took the form of a game (e.g. Simon says) while questioning for older children tended to be more factually based. Children's enthusiasm for such evaluation varied according to the topic being covered and the time of day. If the lesson caught their imagination, they invariably clamoured and competed against one another to give the teacher the answers. When they were visibly uninterested in the lesson, the teachers admonished them for not paying attention, 'being asleep' or making no effort.

Whether or not children were being evaluated formally or informally, the teachers' responses to their performance was invariably public. They praised them for good work and admonished them for poor work:

> 'Very neat work here Lisa'
> 'Stephen, I must compliment you on your work'
> 'Oh I'm very disappointed in that work'
> 'God! Imagine you didn't know that'

The fact that so much evaluation is done publicly in the classroom enhances the power of the teacher in regulating children's behaviour. Observational data also notes how teachers use evaluation as a form of control – reminding children who are inattentive that they will be tested on the topic being covered, or directly asking them questions to check if they are listening:

> I hope everyone is listening, as there will be an oral test on this tomorrow and a written test on Friday (grade 5 teacher, Hillview).

How children experience evaluation

This section explores the children's perception of the formal evaluation of their work through the combined analysis of questionnaire and interview data. A number of themes are explored, related to general attitudes toward being tested, attitudes toward school reports and attitudes toward parent/teacher meetings.

Children's attitudes toward being tested in school

When asked to comment on being evaluated and tested by teachers in school, children revealed ambiguous responses that were influenced by their age and social class. In relation to views on the teacher checking their written work, for example, the younger children were significantly more positive (P<.0001), indicating that this made them feel proud. Further, working class children were more positive than middle class children about having their work checked (P<.05). These differences could be explained by teachers' less pressured orientation toward formal learning with these groups (as highlighted in Chapter 3) and perhaps a greater inclination to praise, entice and encourage these children in their completion of formal learning tasks. The greater expectations and demands made of older children generally and specifically middle class children may be communicated by teachers, evidencing a more serious attitude toward evaluation procedures and stressing the implications of school performance for long term life chances. Such an interpretation is supported by the analysis of the reasons given by the children for their attitudes toward teachers checking their work, as indicated in Table 6.1 below:

Table 6.1 Reasons for children's attitudes to teacher checking their work

Reasons given	N	%
I might get something wrong	38	28.6
I know that I get everything right	38	28.6
The teacher always helps me	20	15.0
I'm not afraid of the teacher	11	8.3
No answer	26	19.5
Totals	133	100.0

The table highlights the variety of discourses children draw on in stating their views, related principally to getting work right or wrong and as viewing the teacher as supportive (as one who helps) or as being defensive. While younger children and girls expressed most confidence about getting things 'right', middle class and older children were most likely to draw on a negative discourse concerning teacher evaluation, fearing they would get their work wrong or stating defensively that they were not afraid of the teacher. Comments during the course of interviews lend support to the pattern found:

> I worry really only about my Irish... other than that I do my work and usually get it right... I feel happiest if I'm talking and the teacher goes: 'are you finished your work?' and I can go 'Yeah I am'... and then she's really sickened... she thinks you are talking and that you're not going to have your work done (grade 5 boy, Churchfield)

> I don't mind the teacher looking at me work cos she has to know how you're doing (grade 5 girl, Parkway)

Testing appeared to be a common feature of classroom life, and over 90% of children agreed that they were tested a lot in school. Once again, however, it was the older children who held the most ambiguous attitudes toward such testing (P<.001) and were more likely to say they were 'nervous' about being tested in school. Not surprisingly, ability level[4] was also found to be significantly associated with attitudes to tests (p<.05), with children who perceived themselves to be less clever more negative in their attitudes than their higher ability counterparts in their attitudes to tests. The contrast in attitudes to tests is borne out in interview data:

> Tests wreck me fucking head... I don't learn them cos they are a waste of time... they're not getting you anywhere... seriously you don't need them (grade 5 boy, Parkway)

> Tests are good... I love them... it tests your brain and it proves that what you are told to do outside school you can study yourself. (grade 5 girl, Churchfield)

Children's perceptions of the reasons for tests drew primarily on themes related to viewing them as an aid to learning, for disciplinary purposes to check attentiveness and to check for 'cleverness', as indicated in Table 6.2 opposite.

Such patterns reflect the views held by teachers that tests were used mainly for diagnostic purposes (to classify children as well as support them in their learning) and as a form of control.

During the interviews, several issues emerged about being tested at school that were not raised in the questionnaires. The first relates to children's understanding that tests are an important preparation for the future, either moving into a higher grade or for exams in secondary school. This instrumental discourse on evaluation was mainly evident in the views expressed by older children in the study:

> Tests are good cos it kind of prepares children for the junior cert[5] and they can't go up and ask the teacher if they are stuck (grade 5 girl, Churchfield)

> You have to have your mind tested all the time cos then you won't forget things... and you can show if your good enough to

Table 6.2 Summary table of children's perceptions of why they are tested in school

Why Teachers Give Tests	Agree		Don't Know		Disagree		No Answer		Totals	
	N	%	N	%	N	%	N	%	N	%
To check for cleverness	87	65.4	18	13.5	21	15.8	7	5.3	133	100.0
As a form of punishment	11	8.3	23	17.3	92	69.9	7	5.3	133	100.0
To help me learn	100	75.2	18	13.5	8	6.0	7	5.3	133	100.0
To check who was listening	70	50.4	28	21.1	28	21.1	7	5.3	133	100.0
To keep children quiet	24	18.0	24	18.0	75	56.4	7	5.3	133	100.0

> go into 6th class or secondary... you have even bigger tests there (grade 5 girl, Parkway)

These views parallel those that emerged during the course of teacher interviews, when teachers emphasise the importance of tests in preparing children for the future:

> I think tests are important because I like to know how the children are doing and you can see their progress over time... they prepare children as well for doing entrance exams[6] and tests in secondary school (grade 5 teacher, Churchfield)

Emphasis on preparation for the future leads teachers to give more frequent tests in some subjects than others, much to the annoyance of some children:

> Our teacher has a thing about tests... especially maths tests... that's all she ever gives us... maths maths maths... she's obsessed with them (grade 5 girl, Hillview)

> English is the most we get tests in and maths as well... and she makes us repeat them... even if we get everything right (grade 5 boy, Churchfield)

The frequency of testing in these areas highlights the emphasis in the education system on learning within the logical/mathematical and linguistic spheres (Gardner, 1993 and 1999) and conveys to children their importance over and above other subject areas (as discussed in Chapter 2). However, teachers soften the frustration at having to do tests and being constantly under evaluation by allocating rewards such as reduced homework, watching a video, awarding stars, thus highlighting the negotiated context of school practice:

> Rewards for work are good cos it encourages children to work harder... I think it's brilliant... the spellings standard has gone up since last year... they are fair cos if children work hard enough they will get them. (grade 5 girl, Churchfield)

> If you do your work good you get points and that's good cos if you get 15 points you get a homework pass... that's deadly that is and sometimes you might get to see a video or a trip (grade 5 boy, Parkway)

It is also worth noting, however, the vulnerability teachers feel in relation to evaluation patterns. Teachers feel a sense of accomplishment or defeat, pride or despair in their work efforts through the progress and performance of their students. They compare and contrast such performance against national averages, or against previous test results, as the following discussion between two teachers in Hillview indicates:

> Teacher 1: I enjoy doing them and seeing if my class are doing as well as the national average

> Teacher 2: Well that's okay if your class are doing well... if the test is very hard and a child scores a three that you thought should be a five or six and you think 'oh God' and you do feel a certain loss of self confidence (Discussion between 2nd and grade 5 teachers, Hillview)

Children's attitudes toward school reports

The compilation of reports at the end of the school year and sending them to parents is another important aspect of school evaluation. While most children were positively disposed to this method of evaluation (72% stated they felt 'fine' about school reports), the most positive attitudes were held by younger children ($P<.01$) and children who perceived themselves as being clever ($P<.05$):

> I feel pretty good about reports because I always get a perfect report (grade 5 boy, Churchfield)

> I feel nervous, shivery and lovely when I get my report (grade 2 girl, Hillview)

The significance of reports to the children was evident from the way many, mostly girls, could recite exactly what had been written about them in their previous year's report:

> I love them... I got: 'Mary is an outstanding pupil who works to a very high standard' (grade 5 girl, Churchfield)

> I usually get on my reports: 'Jackie is always excellent but sometimes can be a bit giddy' (grade 5 girl, Parkway)

> My reports have been getting better but the comment usually says: 'Desmond argues a lot with decisions' (grade 5 boy, Hillview)

Such comments highlight the emphasis teachers place on values related to effort, politeness, attentiveness, neatness and having a positive attitude in school. The children's ability to recall the comments so precisely also suggests the finality of teacher judgements in the children's own minds, enhancing their significance in the formation of children's own constructions of their academic/school identities.

Not all children accepted teacher judgements, however, and a minority were critical of the lack of individuality evident in the reports:

> Usually my report... and I'm not bragging or anything ... it says: 'she's a very good girl and popular with her friends'... I think she wrote that on everyone's report... but teachers don't really know if you are popular or not (grade 5, Hillview)

The compilation of reports is a clear example of how teachers exercise power in school. Because reports are compiled primarily for exchange between adults (teachers to parents) and yet are about children, they are an important device in adult surveillance of children. Children's nervousness over reports stems from the awareness of this surveillance and for some, especially boys, the fear of rebuke if their report is poor:

> When I got a bad school report my da didn't touch me cos he didn't know about it but when my ma came in she started yelling at me (grade 5 boy, Parkway)

> I don't like them cos my mam and dad always give out to me after them (grade 5 boy, Churchfield)

Attitudes toward parent/teacher meetings

Parent/teacher meetings are another important surveillance strategy in schools. While a majority of children expressed positive views about parent/teacher meetings (52%), their views are more ambiguous than about school reports, with almost 40% stating they felt nervous about them. There were no significant associations with gender, class level, social class or perception of ability. If children felt positive about such meetings, this tended to be because they accepted the rights of adults to meet and discuss the children's progress and because they felt they had nothing to fear from such an exchange:

> We do be at home baby-sitting when there's a parent/teacher meeting... children aren't allowed cos it's private between the teacher and your ma... your ma might come home and tell you a different story (grade 5 girl, Parkway)

> It's good for parents to find out how good you are and it's good for them to meet the teacher (grade 5 girl, Churchfield)

As with reports, the children who disliked parent/teacher meetings feared a negative review of their school performance:

> I feel sad about them because I think the teacher is going to tell my parents that I have been bold (grade 2 Parkway)

Many children support the view that children should be excluded from such meetings, precisely because they are nervous about what might be said about them:

> I do be shivering for the meetings... we shouldn't be there cos the teacher wouldn't be able to say how bad you are... but I would like to see my ma's expression to see if she was happy or disappointed (grade 5 girl, Hillview)

A number of boys mentioned being afraid such meetings would be used to rebuke them publicly:

> Oh I'd hate to be there cos if you're bad one day they exaggerate it and then they'd say (pointing finger): 'you did this and you did that' like you were doing it for hours (grade 5 boy, Parkway)

> I wouldn't like to be at one cos if you were getting into trouble they'd be both at you... the teacher and the parents together at the same time (grade 5 boy, Churchfield)

A minority of children disliked the perceived secrecy surrounding what was said about them and wished to be fully involved:

> I think children would like to know what the teacher said about them... sometimes parents don't tell the truth to you... they say: 'oh the teacher said you were great or marvellous'... but the teacher might have said the opposite... I would like to know if my mum was telling the truth and I would like to tell my family

cos it's mine... they are talking about me (grade 2 girl, Churchfield)

This sense of suspicion towards adults, and specifically teachers, is
also evident in the perception some children hold that teachers try to
impress parents and behave differently at the meetings than they do
in class:

> I don't think she would give out to you during a meeting cos
> your ma is sitting there beside you... she wouldn't throw chalk
> at you or anything... she'd be really nice and say: 'ah how are
> you Martin?'... but in school she's not really like that (grade 5
> boy, Parkway)

The data indicates the vulnerability and threat to self that is implicit
in the evaluative structures of the school. Children's ambiguous
views toward parent-teacher meetings reflect the tension they
experience between fearing adults' judgements yet accepting their
right to judge them. Some want a voice in the making of such
judgements yet fear the threat to self which may arise from doing so.

The values implicit in children's perception of their performance in school

The values that influence children in terms of their work are evident
from the issues that make them feel happy or worried about their
work in school, as illustrated in Table 6.3 below:

Table 6.3: What worries children most about their work

What worries me most:	N	%
Nothing	7	5.3
Failure	69	51.9
Being teased	1	0.8
A subject that is 'hard'	22	16.5
Punishment	3	2.3
That it is untidy	16	12.0
No answer	15	11.3
Total	133	100.0

Fear of failure appears to be the most prominent concern of children,
and older children are most likely to express this concern (P<.001).
Conversely, children identified getting the right answer as making them
feel good about their work in school, as indicated in Table 6.4 below:

Table 6.4: What makes children feel good about their work

What makes me feel good:	N	%
Getting it right	60	45.1
Getting it finished	15	11.3
Particular subject	8	6.0
When it is neat	16	12.0
Being praised	19	14.3
No answer	15	11.3
Totals	133	100.0

A distinction can be made in the children's responses between those that are governed by an awareness of the teacher/adult centred (getting work right, being praised, getting work finished, doing work neatly) and those governed by facets of child culture (doing subjects they enjoy – especially Physical Education). Children who perceived themselves to be very clever or clever were most likely to subscribe to the more adult centred norms in their evaluations of what made them feel happy in school ($p<.01$).

Interview data also indicated that child culture, specifically dynamics related to status and approval from peers, was influential in forming children's attitudes:

> I worry about getting things wrong and then everyone would laugh at me... only some people are laughed at really... but when I get a star... oh yeh I feel on top of the world (grade 5 boy, Parkway)

> If my maths was wrong I don't really like her looking... cos then she speaks out loud and everybody else finds out... they slag you then (grade 5 girl, Churchfield)

The evaluation context of the classroom leads children to compare one another in terms of their ability level but they have mixed views about what enables some to do better than others in school, as indicated in Table 6.5 (page 104).

While a substantial proportion of children feel those who do better are naturally 'clever' (32%), a considerable number feel performance in school is related to 'making an effort' and 'paying attention' (24.8% and 22.6% respectively). These are values which teachers constantly stressed in their day to day work (see chapter 4)

Table 6.5 Children's perception of why some children do better than others in school

Why some children do better:	N	%
They make a big effort	33	24.8
They pay attention	30	22.6
They are clever	43	32.3
They are fast at their work	6	4.5
They are the teachers' pets	3	2.3
No answer	18	13.5
Totals	133	100.0

and indicate the internalisation of an 'adult' voice in children's responses. Comments during the interviews reinforced the views expressed above:

> Some children do better cos they listen and they study... some children just couldn't be bothered (grade 5 girl, Churchfield)

> They do better than others cos their brain is good (grade 5 boy, Hillview)

The interviews also indicated that children were very much aware of who in their class was 'brainy' and who wasn't. As outlined in the observational data, practices which teachers engaged in reinforced these perceptions:

> He's real clever right... and sometimes the teacher asks him to teach us things... and I don't like that... cos then we think we're not so clever... I know we aren't but it makes us feel worse... and if other children see him teaching us and he's the same age as me... uh uh... it's stupid it is (grade 5 boy, Parkway)

The power of teachers' influence on children's perception of their own and other's abilities in the classroom is reinforced by the significant correlation identified ($p<.05$) between teacher assessments of each child's ability and how children classified themselves in academic terms.

Children's perception of the values considered important in school are also evident in their understanding of what makes a teacher like a child. Values related to behaviour and productivity came to the fore in their responses to this question. Forty three per cent of children said that the teacher liked a child because they were engaged in 'good' behaviour and 33% stated that the reason related to their work. Responses were influenced by class level (p<.01), with younger children more likely to emphasise behaviour related issues, while older children mentioned productivity/work related issues, patterns reinforced through the interview data:

> A teacher likes a child when you do your work right... to the perfection of the teacher (grade 5 boy, Churchfield)

> A teacher likes a child when they do their work neatly or do their work right and when you concentrate... when you do work work work work and more work work (grade 5 girl, Churchfield)

The impact of the judgements about children made by teachers in light of these norms is evident from the highly ambiguous responses children gave when asked if they felt the teacher liked them. Over 44% stated that the teacher only liked them sometimes and 15% said the teacher never liked them. Once again, the most positive perception of teacher/pupil relationships appeared to be held by younger children and girls, suggesting their stronger affiliation to the ideal type pupil (behaves and learns well) than by older children and boys (P<.001 in each instance).

When asked why they felt they were liked/disliked by the teachers, children again drew on discourses related to productivity (work effort) and behaviour in their responses:

> She likes me sometimes... when I get all my work done and do it neatly... and she doesn't like me when I'm lazy and only get one sum done (grade 5 girl, Churchfield)

Such comments suggest that children perceive their relationship with their teachers to be conditional upon their level of conformity to both social and academic norms. That girls and younger children perceive themselves to be liked by teachers suggests that they see themselves as conforming to such ideals, in contrast to boys and older children who speak of their relations with teachers in more ambivalent terms.

Child culture and being evaluated in school

Children's experience of evaluation in school is not only about how adults evaluate them. A consideration of the dynamics of child culture highlights how children scutinise one another, as shown by their eagerness to find out how everyone does on tests and reports and by their tendency to slag and tease one another over their school performance:

> I'm nervous about the teacher looking at my work cos I don't know what she is going to say... I don't like the other children to find out what I get cos then they just tease you... it is embarrassing sometimes if you have to put up your hand if you got a sum wrong (grade 5 girl, Churchfield)

> I hate when she opens up your copy and reads out the story. It's an Irish story and you have something wrong like a sentence backwards... she'd read that in front of the class[7] and everyone would go duuuuh and you'd be sitting there embarrassed (grade 5 boy, Hillview)

A related issue concerns the annoyance children felt about having to swap their work for correction. They were uncertain whether their classmates would be fair in their corrections and troubled also by the increased exposure of their performance among peers:

> I hate when you have to switch around copies... we have to do that in case we copy... and other people will think you're dumb when they see your marks (grade 5 girl, Parkway)

Children adopt different strategies to deal with the risk to self brought on by such exposure, ranging from feigning indifference at the whole experience (most notable among boys), to seeking the answers from someone else – often with mixed results, as the following conversation reveals:

> *Sarah*: Tests are okay but Louise can be very annoying during maths tests though cos she is always asking me the answer

> *Louise*: But once there's a lot of people up at the teachers' desk I don't like going up and it's kind of hard asking the teacher the same things all the time... it's easier asking Sarah cos I know her so well (grade 5 girls, Churchfield)

Children sometimes bully others to obtain the answers. And they disparage or mock children who are consistently good in school:

> Anto and Grasser and all them... they're always asking me the answers... and they look as if they are getting everything right.. (grade 5 boy, Hillview)

Some children do better than others cos they are licks... Martha... she never got a point off in her whole life... she's not so brainy it's just that she is good... she gets the best fuckin report in the whole school (grade 5 boy, Parkway)

Concluding remarks

It is clear from their recounting of their experiences and views that the children perceive evaluation to be a significant feature of school life and one that is firmly rooted in preparation for the grown up world of work and productivity. For older children especially the experience of evaluation was linked with preparation for future roles and for performance in state examinations in post-primary school. Even if they are critical of the surveillance engendered by continual testing and evaluation and the consequent fear of getting things wrong (views most notable among children of middle class origins), they accept teacher monitoring of their efforts as an inevitable feature of school life. This acceptance is predicated on their appreciation of the benefits of such evaluation, and by implication their present industry and work effort, to their future life chances. Where such investment in time and energy was perceived to be worthless, as a number of older working class boys in Parkway suggested, they tended to dismiss the significance of evaluation in their experience of school. The younger children's attitudes toward evaluation was inherently linked to the interpersonal dimension of their relations with teachers, with the desire for praise, approval and encouragement framing their attitudes and experience. Given the highly public context of most evaluation, it is not surprising that children's views and experience were also framed by their ability level, with those who perceived themselves to be less clever least inclined to speak positively about their experiences of evaluation in school. Children who perceived themselves to be clever spoke about evaluation with some excitement, and welcomed the opportunity for a public display of self in positive terms (through tests, reports, parent/teacher meetings) that brought with it the potential for praise and rewards from significant adults in their lives. Conversely, for children who did not perceive themselves to be clever at school, evaluation brought with it the risk of rebuke and punishment from parents and teachers.

That children classify themselves and others in evaluative terms as good, bold, clever, not so clever, is a significant outcome of the exercise of power and the structuring of childhood in schools. As this and previous chapters have shown, school is a space where children are continually exposed to a series of discourses related to work, learning and social behaviour. Evaluative systems consolidate these discourses, rewarding some forms of behaviour and learning over others and providing children with the context within which they can publicly compare and contrast their behaviour and performance with others in light of these norms. The values the children brought to bear in their work in school revolved primarily around getting it right/avoiding failure, doing it neatly and getting it finished. Perceptions of what made children do well in school reflected these values, and they indicated effort and paying attention as well as natural ability, in their views. The need to get work done correctly and the fear of failure indicates not only an adult zone of influence in children's responses, however. An analysis of the dynamics of child culture highlighted how children also evaluate one another, with teasing over school performance common among children in the study.

While evaluation is experienced by the children as something that is done to them and over which they appear to have little control, the data also highlights how the children actively position themselves with respect to the evaluative structures in school. For those with a strong affiliation to school norms, such positioning involves an acceptance of teacher evaluation, while for others, resistance is the order of the day, achieved through a series of strategies (copying, not completing work) which undermine teacher goals. For most children, however, compliance was the norm, with a ripple of nervousness/excitement at impending evaluations. That children must actively position themselves with respect to their peers is also a significant element in framing their experience of evaluation as they attempt to straddle adult demands for excellence with peer approval and acceptance.

Notes

1 The traditional emphasis on a singular view of ability and of the predominance of mathematical and linguistic abilities in school systems has been queried in light of a more holistic view of human capacity and development. For a fuller discussion of this see for example Howard Gardner (1999/1997/1993) and Sternberg (2002) on multiple intelligence theory and alternate conceptualisations of human intelligence.

2 The teachers themselves typically devised these tests. There is no formalised system of examination and assessment in Irish primary schools, although in order to provide some record of pupil performance, teachers increasingly conduct standardised tests in English and mathematics on an annual basis.

3 The notion of schoolwork as private property is something that is also reinforced through child culture via the competitive thrust of children's interaction with one another over their performance in school. This was referred to in Chapter 2 with reference to children racing against one another to be finished first. The individualist ideology that informs much of the approach to education is part of the structuring of childhood to accord with the values of a capitalist economy and is discussed in Chapter 7.

4 Ability level was determined by the children's own rankings/perception of themselves as 'clever', 'very clever' or 'not so clever' in school.

5 The 'junior cert' is a state examination undertaken typically after three years at post-primary school.

6 The phrase 'entrance examinations' relates to the practice of selective entry by many higher status second level schools through the administration of a system of tests/exams to prospective students prior to being accepted into the school. Focusing primarily on the areas of Irish, English and mathematics they can have a distorting effect on curricular practice toward the senior end of primary school as teachers feel pressured to prepare the children adequately for high performance in them. While entrance exams are now outlawed if used for the purpose of selective entry, many schools still use them as a means of grouping students by ability.

7 Teachers often use this as a pedagogical device as discussed in Chapters 4 and 5.

7
Theorising Child/ Adult Relations

Previous chapters have documented the lived realities of children's lives in school and the salience of power to this experience. We have seen that children are active social beings with the capacity to engage critically with their social and personal environment. Nonetheless this environment brings with it constraints and obligations which are seldom of the children's making and which require them to behave in particular ways. This tension between structure and agency, i.e. the extent to which we are shaped in our behaviour and identity by social rules or whether we actively construct our own path and sense of ourselves, is central to current debates and developments in social theory. This chapter seeks to explore such issues with reference to the structuring of childhood in school. It delves further into the children's views by considering their experience in light of theoretical work on the exercise of power in society and the influence of social structures and individual agency on the formation of personal and social identities. The chapter begins with a brief overview of the work of Foucault and uses his analysis to explore the construction of children as other. Drawing on Giddens' concept of the dialectic of control I also highlight the negotiation of power between adults and children in school. The resulting model draws together the two strands of structure and agency, to illuminate how childhood is structured in school. The model provides a useful framework for examining the structuring of childhood by means of four mechanisms: social relations, curricular, pedagogical and evaluative practice in schools.

Theorising power – constructing the child as other in school

As a prominent post-structuralist Foucault (1979 and 1980) identifies the emergence of distinctively modern modes of power. He examines how power is exercised not through physical coercion and punishment but through the promotion of discourses which define and normalise our behaviour and identities in line with certain ideals. The establishment of institutions such as hospitals, prisons and schools are key elements of social control, corralling segments of the population and subjecting them to a series of interventions. In the process clear dichotomies are created between those who are institutionalised and those who are not, the former determined by the perceived need for intervention and normalisation. The essence of a disciplinary society, for Foucault, is one where attention is geared to the rehabilitation and regulation of those who are outside of the norm. Distinctions are sharpened between the sane and the insane, the sick and the healthy, the virtuous and the criminal and, as in this study, the adult and the child. In modern western societies a defining feature of childhood is compulsory attendance at school, an institution where children are subjected to a series of interventions centred on their formation and control. Through compulsory schooling, children were partitioned from the adult population for the purposes of being normalised, tamed and civilised. They were further subdivided and ranked according to age, gender, social class and perceived ability and subjected to a range of practices, which both defined and regulated their otherness[1]. Such processes clearly demarcated children as other and adults as norm, a viewpoint re-iterated and supported through the rising disciplines of medicine, psychology and education. Children were defined as in a state of in-completeness, to be formed and reformed in terms of the adult ideal. Power in this sense is seen to be productive. In Foucault's words:

> We must cease once and for all to describe the effects of power in negative terms – it excludes, it represses, it censors, it abstracts, it masks, it conceals. In fact power produces, it

produces reality, it produces domains of objects and rituals of truth. The individual and the knowledge that may be gained of him belong to this production (*Ibid.* 1979a: 194)

The focus is on power as it is exercised rather than as it is possessed or acceded to. For Foucault power is all-pervasive, circulating throughout the society with individuals both contributing to and reproducing discourses and norms through their daily behaviour:

> Power must be analysed as something which circulates, or rather as something which only functions in the form of a chain. It is never localised here or there, never in anybody's hands, never appropriated as a commodity or piece of wealth. Power is employed and exercised through a net-like organisation. And not only do individuals circulate between it's threads, they are always in the position of simultaneously undergoing and exercising this power (Foucault, 1980 : 98)

Power is enforced through the use of judgments by teachers, judges, doctors etc. who, through their knowledge and expertise, evaluate reward and normalise behaviour via their institutional practice. In many ways the research described in this book, as other research in the sociology of both education and childhood, is an example of the productive and cyclical aspect of power. In this instance traditional discourses related to the dependence and vulnerability of children are being challenged in favour of discourse which also recognises children's capacities as active agents and their right to greater involvement in decisions which affect their lives.

Criticism has been levelled at Foucault, however, for an overly negative portrayal of the exercise of power (see *inter alia* Barker, 1998; Cousin and Hussain, 1984; Layder, 1997; McNay, 1994). For our purposes, however, his emphasis on power as it is exercised through producing definitions of normality, domains of truth, classifications of other through institutionalised practices sensitises us to the significance of school practices in defining children and childhood in line with dominant discourses of the day. The notion of otherness implicit in the exercise of power, and how this applies to the domain of child/adult relations, had and still has implications for children's perception of their rights and status in school.

In this study the experience of otherness is reflected in the children's comments about many aspects of their school lives. In relation to their curricular experience, for example, the children bemoaned the absence of consultation over what they did in school. The sense of routine and predictability, as well as the pressure to work, is indicative of an analytical pedagogy referred to by Foucault (1979a:152)[2]. From the children's perspective most of what they learned appeared to be centred on the adult world of work and learning rather than their own desire for fun and play:

> We should be allowed choose about PE or going out to the yard... we'd mix work and play more... like at the beginning of the year we could decide the timetable and have an hour of work and an hour break (grade 5 girl, Churchfield)

Curricular experience is intertwined with pedagogical practice and the experience of otherness is conveyed by the comments children make about the general absence of control over their time and space in school. The lack of consultation over the structuring of the timetable reiterates this sense of exclusion and is firmly linked to the greater power of teachers, hence lesser status of children in school:

> Sometimes it feels like a bit like being a robot... like as if the teacher is in the middle of the room with a great big remote control and you have to do everything she says or you will get into trouble (grade 2 girl, Churchfield)

Foucault (1979a) refers to the 'architectural composition of space' as an important aspect of disciplinary power, communicating messages about values and norms. Space as symbolic of the power relations between adults and children in school is reflected in the children's perceived lack of ownership over the school itself, articulated during the course of interviews when they say that the school belongs to the principal; the classroom to the teacher. And the children's acute sense of the difference in the comfort zones available to teachers and pupils, signified to them their lower status in the school[3]. They drew clear analogies between access to well equipped staffrooms and comfortable furniture, and the status of being a 'grown up':

> I wish we had more comfortable chairs... the teachers have them because they are grown ups... they don't respect the children... teachers are respected more by the principal and other teachers (grade 5 Churchfield)[4]

The furniture supplied to the children is another example of the disciplinary technology of schooling, curtailing as it does children's opportunity for movement so as to maximise discipline and learning. The children also recognise that it is designed to reduce their capacity to relax, reinforcing the connection between school and work for pupils, but not necessarily for teachers:

> The teachers have big deadly chairs... they can just sit back (grade 5 boy, Parkway)

> If we get too comfortable on the chair we'd probably doze off or something... or not work that well (5thclass girl, Churchfield)

Rules and regulations are central to the running of schools, setting boundaries to the nature of the children's activity. While the children generally recognised the need for rules, their sense of otherness was again notable in the criticisms they made (especially the older children) over the lack of consultation by the teachers as to what the school rules should be, or in their acknowledgement that children should not be consulted because they were too young, 'bold' and immature and, by implication, different to adults who defined the rules. The fact that teachers did not appear to have their own movement or behaviour curtailed in the same manner reiterated this sense of otherness, causing some children to question teacher authority. As one older boy in Parkway said:

> The teachers are allowed smoke, they're allowed walk around the classroom whenever they want, they're allowed talk whenever they want, they're allowed have cups of tea in the middle of school when we are doing our work and that's not fair cos we are not allowed even have a sandwich and if they don't bring in their lunch they can send someone over to the shop

For most children in the study, being a grown up implied being the boss, with the right to behave and do as one pleased. In contrast, being a child was equated with being curtailed, constrained and often not taken seriously because of their child status:

> The children have the least power cos they're not allowed do anything, say what they want, do what they want... the principal has the most power and the teachers... they're grown up so they're meant to be the bosses (grade 5 boy, Parkway)

> When adults are treated unfairly they stand up and object to it... but they don't kinda take children seriously... they think they are just messing or looking for attention (grade 5 girl, Churchfield)

However the sense of otherness as a child in school is not only communicated through the dynamics of power and control between teachers and pupils. It is also experienced in the domain of peer relations. A whole range of practices and discourses exclude children from friendship groups evoking a sense of not belonging and being different. Such exclusionary practices are significant normalising tendencies in peer culture itself and are typically fuelled by discourses related to gender, social class, dis/ability, ethnicity, and sexuality (Connolly, 1998; Lodge and Flynn, 2001; Thorne, 1993; Troyna and Hatcher, 1992). These dynamics of inclusion and exclusion in peer culture connect with the normalising tendencies in teacher/pupil relations. The normative judgements made by teachers regarding gender, ability, ethnicity and so on provide a context in which children become ranked as bright, weak, smart, giddy and troublesome. Interviews with the children indicated how sensitive they were to teacher judgements, reflected for example in their ability to repeat the details on their annual report cards:

> 'I got: Mary is an outstanding pupil who works to a very high standard'

> 'I usually get on my reports: Jackie is always excellent but sometimes can be a bit giddy' (Grade 5 girls Hillview and Parkway)

Categorising children's ability and their behaviour in this way can be used as a basis for teasing, as well as a marker of who was included or excluded in friendship groupings.

The affective dimension of teacher/pupil relations should not be forgotten, however, and in spite of the children's misgivings about their status in school as other, many spoke positively about their personal relationships with their teachers, particularly those who acknowledged the children's world, bringing fun into teaching and learning and being fair and consistent in the application of school rules. While teachers appear from the children's perspective to be the power holders in the school, the interviews with teachers themselves indicated that they were not entirely comfortable with the manner in which they structured children's school experience, a finding reported in other studies in the field (Hargreaves, 2000; Tirri and Poulinatha, 2000). When given the opportunity to reflect on their practice, the teachers spoke of their frustration at working with large groups of children. They also spoke of how the affective dimension of their role, which seeks to nurture, care for and support children's learning in all aspects, was continually undermined by shortage of space and absence of resources, including time itself. In each area we talked about, whether it was pedagogical or curricular practices, the use of evaluation systems or the nature of social relations with children, the teachers, especially those teaching senior classes, said how they would do things differently if given a free rein:

> I would like bigger rooms... I haven't got room to do the things I'd like to do so I don't bother... like a reading corner... I'd love to have those little areas... have the children have space just for chairs, not desks and have desks up against the walls so they could work there if they need it and have extra space for project work and art (grade 5 teacher, Parkway)

> I would love to spend more time doing music, art and drama... this is my first time having grade 5 in a long time and you automatically have to take on a different role cos suddenly everything is very serious and a lot of the fun goes out of it (grade 5 teacher Hillview)

Discourse, power and schooling

The tension between these teachers' views and their practice, along with the children's accounts of their school experience indicate a broader tension between the various discourses which support and underlie schooling and education. In his analysis, Foucault (1979a: 194) speaks of the 'domains of truth' or discourses that both derive from and contribute to the exercise of power in a range of social institutions. Two such discourses are pertinent to our analyses, economic discourse and child-centred discourse.

Economic discourse permeates school practice through the emphasis that is placed on schooling as a preparation of children for their future adult working lives. The massive investment in education by governments derives from this link, with greater investment in Ireland geared toward those aspects of the education system which accord with the labour market[6]. What gives legitimacy to the manner in which schools are organised, and by implication to the construction of children as other, is this connection between children's school labour[7] and economic prosperity. The curtailment of children in time and space through compulsory schooling, the pressure to work, the exercise of normative judgments which value and reward some forms of learning over others and the constant surveillance of children's behaviour are all geared toward the maximisation of children's productivity to the ultimate benefit of the economy[8].

The influence of economic discourse is evident in the way teachers and children talk about school. The teachers spoke about the demands of the curriculum, the pressured nature of the timetable and about their awareness of having to prepare children for entry to secondary level schooling and university by instilling the basics into them:

> It seems to filter down from university... academic subjects dictate what the curriculum will be in secondary school and then primary school... you feel if you don't do so much now they will lose out when they go to secondary school (grade 5 teacher, Hillview)

The teachers' pedagogical practice was immersed in commentary that emphasised the importance of discipline and concentration in learning and the promotion of a strong work ethic. Classifications of the children into bright, weak, chatty, quiet, were reinforced through formal and informal evaluation systems, as teachers juggled the demands of the curriculum with the need for crowd control. Children were at all times being watched, monitored and controlled. As one teacher said:

> I have my desk at the top because it's beside the blackboard and I can see all the children but I have had it at the back so the children couldn't see me but I could see them (grade 2 teacher Parkway)

In their interviews the children spoke frequently about the control and surveillance that permeated their school lives, resonating with Foucault's (1979a:140) concept of 'the gaze':

> I'd put the teachers' desk as far away as possible... cos she's watching your every move... every time you even look in your bag she's watching over you... and if ye want to get a headstart in your homework she sees you (grade 5 girl, Hillview)

> I do think the teacher has eyes at the back of her head cos when she's out of the room she knows stuff that happened and even if she's sitting at her desk she is looking out the side of her eye to see who is even whispering (grade 2 girl, Churchfield)

The impact of economic discourse on the children was evident in a number of respects. They had a definite understanding of what was important and valued in their education, and drew distinctions between the 'real' learning of Irish, English and mathematics as opposed to the 'fun' learning of subjects such as physical education, music and art. They were also quite clear about the purposes of education defining it in mainly instrumental terms. They needed to go to school in order to get a good education, which they saw as a necessary prerequisite for adult employment. Acceptance of teacher authority and control was predicated on the economic functionality of education: to make sacrifices today was to obtain benefit at some time in the future[9]. They also had a clear understanding of the ideal pupil – as one who is obedient, works hard, is restrained and self-controlled:

> A teacher likes a child when they do their work neatly or do their work right and when they concentrate... when you do work, work and more work work work (grade 5 girl, Churchfield)

There is, however, a parallel discourse informing primary school practice, namely child centredness[10]. This softens the more rigid and authoritarian approach to schooling that economic discourse can imply. While the focus on the maximisation of individual talent in child centred approaches accords neatly with economic goals, the thrust of teacher/pupil relations is geared toward a benevolent paternalism which focuses on sensitivity to children's needs and wants (Devine, 1999). In the study this paternalism was most apparent in the junior classes, where teachers were perceived by the children and perceived themselves to be kinder, less strict and more 'mammy like' in their interactions with the younger children. However this was less evident with the older children as the pressure for academic achievement gave rise to more rigid work routines. In spite of the more caring dimension of such discourse, however, child centred approaches can reinforce the notion of children as other in their relations with adults, emphasising needs over rights and undermining children's own capacities for critical reflection and judgment[11]. In relation to the exercise of power between adults and children in school, teachers often justified the level of control exercised over children's time and space with reference to such discourse, citing children's need for order and consistency, for discipline and direction. This was frequently expressed by teachers and principals who found it difficult to comprehend the concept of children as co-decision makers in, for example, the organisation of school:

> At this age there should be little consultation... I don't think they are mature enough... I mean if they had their way they'd be out playing games twenty four hours a day and they wouldn't see the importance of academic achievement and mucking under doing maths or whatever... so these are decisions you have to make for them (Principal, Parkway)

Others dismissed decision-making by children as a potential threat to teacher authority or as something to be encouraged only as a form of reward for good behaviour:

> I don't see there is a place for the children to be telling or ruling the school at this stage... I think where will it ever end this thing of giving them their say and they also have to learn how to make the right decision and be given examples of the right decision... they should participate in decisions as a privilege rather than of right and if it suits the running of the school (grade 2 teacher, Churchfield)

As some of the children saw it, especially those in the senior classes, such views were a denial of children's rights and a reluctance to take the children's views seriously:

> The children should be allowed make the rules sometimes... well not make them but have their say in it... have their opinion... I suppose the teachers would think the children would have lots of fights and they would be bold (grade 5 girl Hillview)

Foucault's analysis of power in modern society provides a valuable framework for analysing relations of power between adults and children. His emphasis on capillary power (*Ibid*: 1980:96), i.e. power at the extremities as it is practiced in social institutions, directs attention to how power is exercised between adults and children in schools. His analysis is useful in sensitising us to the significance of institutionalised practices in constructing children as other in their relations with adults in school and of the role of discourse (in this instance economic and child centred discourse) in promoting and legitimising such practice. Through their experience of schooling, children form identities as pupils – with all this implies in terms of obedience, work effort, restraint and self-control.

The dialectic of control in child/adult relations

There is a danger that such analysis may portray children as objects, unquestioningly subject to administrative and social control. Children, however, are capable of both submitting to and exercising power in their relations with adults in schools. Learning, the main goal of teachers, is predicated on the compliance and attention of learners. My study shows how teachers regularly negotiated with children in order to maintain their focus and attention during class time. The use of rewards and the withholding of sanctions were observed in all the classrooms. Teachers cajoled and encouraged their students toward maximum learning in school, as the following excerpts from field diary notes illustrate:

> 'Stop the talking or I'm going to separate you'
> 'I'm going to have to start putting names on the blackboard'
> The next person I catch talking is getting fifty lines'
> 'Amanda! If you don't settle, I'll send a note home'
> 'The more you talk the more sums I write'
> 'Patricia! Next step for you is Mr Monaghan's'

Pollard (1985 and 1996) stresses the importance of developing a working consensus between teachers and pupils as an example of the negotiated character of classroom life. The exercise of power between teachers and pupils is a two way process which gives each party to the interaction some control over its direction. This is what Giddens refers to as the dialectic of control. He asserted:

> However subordinate an actor may be in a social relationship the very fact of involvement in that relationship gives him/her a certain amount of power over the other (*Ibid*: 1979:6)

This is not to suggest that power is always exercised on an equal basis. On the contrary, Giddens suggests that the inherently unequal nature of power relationships derives from the difference in access individuals have to both economic and authoritative resources, the latter involving the capacity to control the time/space, life chances and social interaction of others. As we have seen, teachers enjoy greater access to such resources by virtue of their adult status, controlling children in time and space through their curricular and pedagogical practice, influencing their life chances and setting boundaries to the nature of children's interaction in school. But there are spaces where children carve out zones of influence, for example, wearing their teacher down through continual inattention and indifference to the norms of the school. This was particularly evident in the behaviour of a group of boys in grade 5 in Parkway:

> I was chewing something all morning and your not allowed to eat in class. I was messing and the teacher gave me lines 'I must not chew in class' and I did them 'I must chew in class'. I forgot to put the 'not' in and she was yelling at everyone and looking at me all the time (grade 5 boy Parkway)

One way of understanding children's resistance to adult control is to classify their behavior into regions and examine those regions where children are most likely to resist adult domination. Goffman (1961 and 1971) maintains that the front regions are those where we perform a publicly visible role such as doctor, mother, teacher, pupil, with all the social constraints this implies. Back regions are those spaces where we can shed our public face and behave in a manner that ignores or defies the norms and conventions which are part of our public role. It is in the back regions that individuals are free to remove the façade of the roles and social positions assigned in the front region. In schools the staffroom is an important back region where teachers can relax, dropping the role of teacher. For children an obvious back region is the schoolyard or playground where adults find it impossible to monitor all the behaviour children engage in and where children are free to act in a manner which would be unacceptable as pupil in the classroom. Other back regions include the toilets, corridors, under the desks and behind copybooks.

The existence of back regions in schools provides a necessary outlet for tension that results from continual compliance with and sur-veillance by the teacher. Teachers' toleration of children's more noisy and unruly behaviour in such regions derives from the dialectic of control: they provide pupils with spaces for some auto-nomy in the knowledge that this will facilitate concentration and learning when required. As Giddens says:

> Discipline through surveillance is a potent medium of generating power, but it nonetheless depends upon the more or less continuous compliance of those who are subjects. The achievement of such compliance is it'self a fragile and con-tingent accomplishment... The disciplinary context of the class-room is not just a backdrop to what goes on in the school class: it is mobilised within the dialectic of control (Ibid. 1984: 136)

Although Giddens (1984, 1979) reiterates Foucault's emphasis on the controlling and subjugating aspects of the exercise of power in modern society, his analysis moves beyond considering the exercise of power in terms of domination and subordination alone[12]. He also draws attention to the transformative and change elements of power and the capacity of all individuals to exercise some influence over the interaction process through the dialectic of control. Such analysis is particularly applicable when applied to schools – here teachers and pupils are engaged in a process (teaching and learning) that is effective only in so far as there is some compromise and negotiation over classroom processes.

The struggles for control, the pressures for achievement, the de-mands of the curriculum, the negotiation over learning and work effort identified throughout this study highlight the power struggles that take place in school and classroom life. These tensions and struggles should not be considered as isolated elements of school-ing. The way schools are is largely determined by the values and priorities that exist in relation to education in the broader society, for it is society that establishes goals, and limits what is possible in schools. Thus there are fundamental links between what happens in schools and what takes place in the broader society. This link between micro-practices in the school and the macro level of society is explored in social theory with reference to the concepts of structure and agency.

Structure and agency in children's school experience

In social theory, structure refers to the manner in which society regulates and influences human behaviour through its social organisation. The development of a shared commitment to certain ideals, culture and values is central to such analysis. This commitment is communicated and reinforced through a variety of systems such as education, politics, religious and legal systems. Through immersion into the culture and institutions of the society, individuals develop social identities based on their gender, ethnicity, social class, sexuality and dis/ability. Structural analysis examines the patterning of relationships within each of these categories, for example between men and women, working class and middle class, black and white, locating these patterns in differences in power and position between each of these groups in the broader society.

Applied to the area of child/adult relations, structural analysis examines the social basis of such relations and how interactions between adults and children are structured in line with norms and values that exist in the wider society. Here structure may be understood as the rules and regulations operating in a variety of social institutions, which pre and post date our existence and which continually shape and form behaviour. Such analyses, inspired particularly by the work of Functionalists (e.g. Durkheim, 1956 and 1964; Parsons, 1951 and 1964) and Marxists (e.g. Bowles and Gintis, 1976; Althusseur, 1972) albeit from differing viewpoints, posit a view of the individual as one who is moulded and governed by society. Schools and schooling are seen as central to this process of socialisation and there is a considerable body of sociological literature related to the reproductive and socialising tendencies of schools (e.g. Archer, 1979; Bourdieu, 1996; Bowles and Gintis, 1976; Drudy and Lynch, 1993; Lynch, 1989; Parsons, 1951; Sharp and Green, 1975; Willmott, 2001). A number of important issues emerge from a structural analysis of schooling in terms of the exercise of power between adults and children.

We can begin to identify the rules and regulations governing child/ adult; teacher/pupil relations as structures that shape children's identities in line with dominant norms. Drawing on the work of both Marx and Durkheim, Giddens (1984) identifies structure as the rules and resources which individuals draw on in the course of their daily interaction. Rules may be understood as the discourses and norms which define our behaviour, while resources enable these rules to be translated into practice.[13] Applied to our focus on child/adult relations, adult discourses in relation to children filter into school practice through economic investment in a school system and the authority given to teachers to control the time and space, interaction and life chances of children. These latter areas coincide with curricular, pedagogical, social relation and evaluative practices in school. This is illustrated in Figure 1 below:

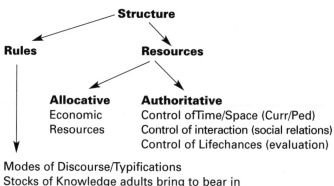

Figure 1: Structures influencing child-adult relations in schools

Although Giddens' theory has been subjected to valid criticisms[14] it is clear that rules and resources, as outlined above, influence practice in schools. The Irish school system, like other education systems, is bound up with the project of modernisation. Children's schooled activities are governed by economic, political, social and religious discourses which define both what it is to be a child and how childhood should be experienced for the greater good of society (Devine, 1999). These discourses form the basis for the rules of schooling, translated into practice through the authoritative resources of teachers. Discourses related to education and learning, and to child development, cut across these discourses, often creating tensions for teachers themselves as they attempt to implement an increasingly diversified curriculum. We have identified two discourses[15] in teacher talk that are relevant to our analysis – child centred and economic discourse, and these may be understood to provide rules for teachers' engagement with their pupils. These discourses inform decisions related to what and how teachers teach, how they interact with pupils and how and what they evaluate in school, issues explored in Chapters 2 through to 6. We have also seen that from the children's perspectives, the school experience is structured in terms of compliance, individualism, self-discipline and hard work, with those outside of this norm subject to a range of normalising practices that strive to bring them in line with school goals. Their experience accords with the requirements and values of a society structured around a modern capitalist economy. In the merging of adult discourse with children's experience, power is exercised, positioning children as other in school and influencing how they think of themselves as persons with particular identities.

The importance of agency

We have also seen, however, that children do not conform totally to teacher demands but question teacher authority and exercise some influence over classroom processes. Social structures or rules influence what takes place in the classroom but do not totally determine it. Children may be structured as other in school, their lives may be centred on discipline and learning but they do not react to such experience uniformly. As active agents they create their own autonomous spaces where they can be more firmly in control. Thus a parallel world of child culture co-exists with that of the child/adult world, providing children with the opportunity, as discussed in Chapter 2, to undermine the rules and constraints that govern their behaviour when in the company of adults. As one girl in Churchfield said:

> Everybody has to break the no running rule at least one time... it's just the way children are... we play chasing and we run... (*to researcher*: don't tell the teachers)... everybody has to break a rule in their life (Grade 2).

Child culture itself is not uniform and children actively locate themselves with one another on the basis of their gender, ethnicity, social class, age and dis/ability. In the ongoing flow of classroom life, children jostle and compete with one another for status, affiliation and belonging, positioning themselves with peers on the basis of their affiliation and/or resistance to dominant school norms (Davies, 1982 and 1990; Pollard, 1985; Pollard and Filer, 1999, Willis, 1977; Woods, 1990). They also position themselves with respect to their teachers. The complexity of response that is required to marry the adult and child worlds is reflected in the commentary of one child:

> You have to keep up your reputation... you can't be a goody goody either... like always telling and always getting your work right, asking questions, not breaking the rules (grade 5 boy, Churchfield)

It would be a mistake, though, to interpret children's agency in school solely in terms of resistance to or acceptance of adult control. The influence and change children exert over teacher practice in the front regions of school life is also an example of their agency as they challenge the very discourses teachers bring to their classroom practice. Time in school is also time adults spend with children when they are influenced, formed and reformed by the myriad of responses and complexities children themselves bring to the school process. As one class teacher in Parkway stated:

> I've changed an awful lot... I would have been much more aggressive toward the children as a way of keeping discipline... not as conscious of how the children felt... when you have a difficult class you have to change your style... there's less conflict and the children are happier which is better in the long run

The continual effort and persistence children display in their learning is also evidence of their capacities as active agents. They may be critical of a lot of their learning experiences in school, especially when the work is hard or of a routine nature[16], but nonetheless children's constant engagement with new material challenges them to exercise their judgement and skills in myriad ways:

> I like reading and sums... your teacher calls you up to do your reading and when you do loads of pages you get to finish the book (grade 2 girl Parkway)

> Tests are good... I love them... it tests your brain and it proves that what you are told to do outside of school you can study yourself (grade 5 girl, Churchfield)

As reflective agents children know what they do and why they do it. Their compliance or rejection of school norms is based on an active appreciation of the value of schooling to their future lives. For most, schooling is deemed to be a fact of life, taken for granted if not entirely approved of, in the knowledge that it will prove useful for examination results, job prospects and life generally. For a minority, continual resistance is the order of the day, predicated on these children's reasoned assumptions that schooling has little relevance to their present or long-term lives.

The depiction of children's active management of their school lives coincides with recent work related to the development and formation of personal and social identity. With its origins in the work of Cooley (1902) and Mead (1972) and later influences by Vygotsky (1978 and 1999) and Foucault (1979 and 1982), social constructivism emphasises the active contribution of the person to her sense of identity, sorting and selecting from the range of rules, values and beliefs which prevail in society. While the individual, through social interaction, acquires rules of the culture, social constructivists insist that individuals are both created by and manipulators of such culture, striving to maintain a positive sense of self through their interactions with others.

For the school-going child, an added dimension to such interaction is the highly ambiguous context of school, in which evaluation by teachers and comparisons with peers ensures that the child's self image is constantly being challenged and questioned. As one boy in Parkway said: 'I worry about getting things wrong and then everyone will laugh at me'. The risk to self implied in his comment is part and parcel of learning in a public environment and children develop a range of strategies to cope and retain a positive self image. The strategies they use include copying or getting help from others, forgetting work, adopting delaying tactics and feigning general indifference to schooling and achievement. This latter was especially notable among boys in the study and part of the culture of masculinity in male peer groups in school (Connell, 1995; Connnolly,

1998; Mac an Ghaill, 1994). So we can see how children actively engage with the culture of school, accepting some aspects and rejecting others, in a complex interplay between appeals to adult (parent and teacher) and peer norms.

A number of important issues emerge from this analysis. First, identity is socially constructed, derived from the range of discourses to which the individual is exposed and consequently discourses relating to childhood will influence the perceptions children have of themselves. The norms, discourses and resources governing child/ adult relations provide the context through which children define themselves, as they learn to function in social life. Second, schools as institutions both derive from and are indicative of the discourses and norms governing child/adult relations in modern societies and thus play a central role in both the definition and experience of modern childhood. In terms of their experience of school, the analysis suggests that children actively position themselves with respect to these structural influences, defining themselves and being defined by the range of discourses to which they are exposed on a daily basis in schools. However, children define themselves in terms of their relations not only with adults but also with their peers, in terms of their gender, social class, ethnicity dis/ability etc. As active agents they position themselves with respect to each of these areas, defining their identities and shaping their behaviour according to their own experiences. The manner of such positioning will be influenced by the interrelation between both cognitive and social/ socio-historical factors, as well as unconscious (e.g. retaining a positive sense of self) and conscious influences.

The structuring of childhood in school

Taking account of the analysis of the structure/agency dialectic in social interaction and the significance of power in this process, we can bring together a model that provides a useful framework for interpreting the structuring of childhood in school. The model comprises four parts related to structure, agency, power and practice and is detailed in Figure 2 below:

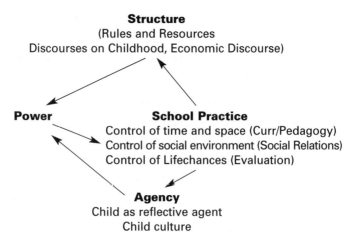

Figure 2: Power circulates: a model of the interrelationship between structure, power and agency in school practice

This framework illustrates how structures representing discourses of childhood in society influence school practice by means of the level and nature of control exercised over children's time and space, their social environment and their life chances. Each of these areas of control is typically reflected in the curricular, pedagogical, social relational and evaluative practices in schools as outlined in Chapters 2 to 6. School practice in turn influences children's construction of themselves as children, in terms of their role and positioning as individuals in school. However, this positioning is an active process. Children reflect, react and accommodate to such practices, incorporating them into their own sense of self. Power is exercised in this process, the level of transformation or reproduction of existing practices depending on the operation of the dialectic of control and the degree of latitude allowed to both teachers and children in the interpretation of classroom practice. Child culture also figures predominantly in children's agency, as they filter their interactions with teachers through the lens of their peers. And this culture enables children to participate in a social world relatively free from adult surveillance, a world that is made up of its own rules and regulations which structure and frame children's behaviour and their identification with one another.

We can apply the model to each of the areas of school practice that formed the focus of research for this book. Table 1 (see page 132) summarises the main findings in line with the theoretical categories identified in the model.

The dimension of power is central to the connections between each of the categories represented in the table. Power is exercised in each instance through the translation of dominant discourses into social relational, curricular, pedagogical and evaluative practices that teachers draw upon in their daily practice. Through the exercise of such power children construct a sense of themselves as other in their relations with adults in school. While this otherness is signalled in the compulsory placement of children in school, it is communicated in practice through the extensive control exercised in all aspects of their school lives. The absence of consultation with children over the nature of their school experience contributes greatly to this sense of otherness. They express their resistances passively through their bodies rather than actively through direct forms of participation and consultation in matters which affect them. As one teacher observed:

> I think we listen without consciously thinking we are listening... like you start off on a Monday morning with an Irish lesson and you think ah they're asleep we'll move on to something else... they're showing passively they're not ready for this and so you go on, in that kind of way, subconsciously even (grade 5 teacher Hillview)

This is the subjugated effect of power. Both teachers and children frequently rationalise their reality by appealing to the long-term goals of academic achievement as benefiting the children's adult working lives. This is the cycle of power Foucault refers to: the micro practices in the school both draw upon and contribute to the macro economic level in the society in a continual feedback loop. Adjustments in practice are made in light of new knowledge about schooling, education, the needs of the economy and the needs of children. If children are given the opportunity to participate overtly in this cycle by exercising their voices, new forms of knowledge and understanding about schooling can emerge that may influence and change practice in schools and classrooms. This is the productive aspect of power that brings with it challenges, opportunities and

	Structure (Rules: Discourses/Norms)	Institutionalised Practice	Agency/ Children's construction of selves
Social Relations	Economic discourse positions children as other, in need of compulsory schooling. Teachers enter relations with pupils with view to appropriate normalisation in line with economic ideals. Child centred discourses position children in terms of their needs for protection, care and age appropriate education.	Teacher/pupil relations marked by authority, care and control, with age differentiated interactions. Little concept of children's rights or capacities for shared decision making in school and classroom activities. Tension between control and personal relationship dimensions of teachers' work fuelled by context of restrictive funding for primary education.	Children perceive themselves as subordinate to teachers. Form own social world (child culture) that counterbalances absence of autonomy in relations with teachers. Varies by gender, age, ethnicity, ability and social class. Influences level of resistance to or accommodation of teacher control.
Curriculum	Economic discourse: school learning defined as preparation for future adult role. Some forms of learning prioritised over others. Child centred discourse asserts sensitivity to children's needs in learning.	Control of time and space through standardised curriculum. Timetable structures children's activity into work time and play time. Reflects valuing some subjects as more important than others. Little consultation with children.	Tension between fun and real learning, with latter defined as work. Resist, accept or accommodate to the curriculum dependent on affiliation to long term goals of work and career.
Pedagogy	Discourses stress norms related to self, interaction with others and work. Children perceived to require discipline, encouragement and control.	Extensive control systems centred on signals, voice, teacher physical presence, control of the body, rules and regulations, reward and punishment; negotiation where necessary but not of right.	Contrasting constructions of self as dependent/in need of protection versus having a right to question level of control exercised. Latter influenced by gender, social class and age level as well as child culture in their attempts to steer a balance between adult and peer approval.
Evaluation	Economic discourse: school learning defined as preparation for future adult role. Need for accreditation and classification of children by ability and performance.	Exercise of normative judgments based on work effort and general social demeanor through system of formal and informal evaluation structures.	Clear classification of self in ability terms. Protection of emerging self-image through host of strategies, from working hard to feigning indifference.

risks for all those involved. The final chapter considers these issues with specific reference to the policy implications of the study.

Notes

1 The establishment of schools in the 19th century facilitated the study of children as a group, giving rise to discourses on childhood in the fields of psychology, sociology, education and medicine. New relations of power between adults and children emerged which could not have developed without the production, circulation and functioning of a discourse (Foucault, 1980: 93). With the rise of psychology as a scientific discipline in the first half of the 20th century, theories of child development abounded, with the focus on the gradual maturation of the child through a logical sequence of development. Psychoanalytical theory has given rise to further discourse on childhood, in what is termed as the 'unconscious child' (James *et al*, 1998) with the work of Freud in particular setting the foundations for considering childhood in retrospect as having an inordinate influence on drives and motivations in adulthood. Recent analyses informed by both psychological and sociological perspectives challenges traditional views about children and childhood advancing a discourse which stresses the agency and rights of children (James *et al*, 1998; Mayall, 2002; Morrow, 1995; Qvortrup *et al*, 1994). These new discourses, of which this book is one example, form an essential part of the power knowledge circuit in society, with a whole new knowledge base developing that seeks to augment the status of children relative to adults in society.

2 For Foucault (1979), an analytical pedagogy implies the promotion of regularity and rhythm in the school day and the standardisation of all procedures, which are analysed to the minutist detail. The productive aspect of such disciplinary techniques is evident in the synthesis of the entire body that is required to perform tasks such as handwriting – with a detailed code of behaviour specified from 'the points of the feet to the tip of the index finger' (*Ibid*:152). This control of the body is mirrored by the control of time through the timetable. Efficiency and non-idleness characterise the timetable, consolidating the ideal of disciplinary perfection, promoting the body's utility while rendering it more docile.

3 This was something I had to guard against in my own positioning during field observation. Teachers, by way of being polite and supportive, invariably sought to find 'comfortable seating' for me during classroom visit's. However I always insisted on using the children's desks or chairs to sit in, thus communicating to the children that I was not quite like other adults in the school.

4 What is important to note in this comment, which was not simply an isolated viewpoint but one expressed by many children in the study, is the association between the organisation of space (in this instance the availability of comfortable seating) and the status of being 'grown up' and by implication the other status of the children. The issue of respect generally for children is one over which there was some dispute among the children, as it crossed over other dynamics in the teacher/pupil relationship related to concern, the commitment to care and being helpful and supportive to children.

5 Lortie (1975) speaks of this affective dimension as providing the psychic rewards of teaching and its significance is the retention of teachers in the classroom in spite of often adverse working conditions.

6 There has been considerable controversy in Ireland in recent years over the regressive funding of the education system, with greater per capita funding given to the University sector. Primary schooling, while catering to the needs of all citizens in the state, receives the least funding per capita, frequently resulting in large class sizes and an absence of adequate infrastructural development. The regressive funding patterns can also be understood in terms of the 'other' status of younger children whose education is not perceived as valuable as those whose studies tie directly with the demands of the labour market.

7 Qvortrup (1987 and 2001) argues that children's work, their 'school labour', parallels that of adult work given the long-term benefit to the economy.

8 Investment in education is frequently justified on the ground of the long-term gain to the economic development of the society (e.g. Brown and Lauder, 1996; Coleman, 1998; Hartley, 2003). In Ireland, the move to industrialisation in the 1960s led to calls for a more technically proficient and literate population and was reflected in a greater willingness to invest in education. The highly instrumental view of education articulated by influential economists at the time portrayed a view of children as being there to serve the future needs of the industrialising economy. This instrumental orientation mirrored the views of parents who saw education as a means of improving the lifechances of their children (Devine, 1999). State policy geared toward the expansion of the education system in the 1960's has been directly linked to the production of the 'Celtic Tiger Economy' of the 1990s.

9 Not surprisingly, observational data indicated that the greatest challenges to teacher authority came from a group of boys in working class Parkway who perceived schooling and education to be generally irrelevant to their lives. Their views were in stark contrast to the students in middle class Churchfield, who were well versed in the long-term benefit's of schooling and education.

10 There has been continuing controversy over the meaning and nature of child centred education, with positive analyses offered by Entwistle (1974) and Walkerdine (1984) and more critical approaches reflected in the work of Sharp and Green (1975) and Mayall (1996). For a discussion of child centred approaches with reference to Irish primary teachers see Sugrue (1997).

11 For a fuller discussion of this analysis of child centred approaches to education see for example James, Jencks and Prout (1998), Woodhead (1990) and Blitzer (1991).

12 There is some dispute about the extent to which Foucault's analysis also directs attention to the more positive and transformative aspects of power. See for example McNay (1994), Cousins and Hussain (1984), Peters (2003) for a fuller discussion.

13 Giddens draws together core elements of the main sociological theories into his theory of structuration. At the core of this theory is the tension between structure and agency in our social lives as we modify and interpret out sense of ourselves through social experience. He compartmentalises the rules we follow into two main categories: structures of signification and structures of legitimation. Structures of signification refer predominantly to the understandings and meanings we bring to particular categories or events (i.e discourses, typifications, stocks of knowledge), while structures of legitimation refer to the norms which govern our behaviour (i.e the rules relating to what is approved or disapproved of by the society or community). Applied to our understanding of child-adult relations, structures of signification can refer to the discourses of childhood we draw on – with which we both define and understand what it is to be child. Thus child centred discourse defines children as being innocent and in 'need' of adult protection, guidance and care. Such discourse is legitimated in practice through a series of norms (structures of legitimation) which emphasise sensitivity to children's needs and caring/ protective behaviour toward children.

14 See for example Archer (1990 and 1998), Craib (1992),Layder (1997), Schilling (1992), Willmott (1999).

15 This is not to suggest that these were the only discourses which informed the teachers' practice. There were also elements of religious discourse which drew on Christian values related to community, caring and respect for one another. Particular discourses related to gender, ability and social class were also evident. Each of these discourses articulated through teacher practices and form part of the exercise of power in schools. For a more detailed analysis of the influence of such discourses on school practice see for example the work of Connolly (1998), Lodge and Flynn (2001), Paetcher (1998).

16 See Pollard and Triggs (2000) for a fuller discussion.

8

Redistributing Power in Schools

This book has explored the structuring of childhood through schooling, placing the children's voices at the centre of the analysis. By listening to what they have had to say, we get a sense of how they experience school and how their experience influences their emerging identities. The model outlined in Chapter 7 indicates the links between these voiced experiences and the exercise of power between adults and children in the wider society. This provides, a framework for answering the three questions posed in Chapter:

- How do children experience schooling?

- What does the children's perspective tell us about the exercise of power between adults and children and the structure of childhood through school?

- In what ways do children exercise agency in school?

This chapter provides an outline of the main findings and addresses these questions. It also considers a fourth question by way of overall conclusion.

- How can power be exercised in a manner that empowers children through their greater active involvement in structuring their school experience?

By answering this question, this concluding chapter sets out the implications of the findings for those working in the field of education: practitioners and policy makers. It is clear that children should be key stakeholders in the decision making process in schools, not outsiders looking in. This chapter discusses the discourses related to citizenship and children's rights so as to identify an appropriate framework within which to empower and validate the perspectives of children in primary schools.

How children experience school

When asked what they think about school, the contrast in attitudes between children who have just started and those who are well embedded in the school system is often stark. New recruits to school are generally enthusiastic albeit slightly wary of the challenges and opportunities facing them in their journey through 'big school'. As they move through the school system, however, children's enthusiasm appears to wane; their excitement over learning gives way to mixed feelings related to the familiarity, routine and discipline of schooling. The research described in this book sought to get behind these patterns, talking with, listening to and observing children over the course of a school year. I explored four key areas of school experience: relations with teachers and peers, curriculum, pedagogy and evaluation.

As the children recounted their experiences, common themes emerged across these areas. Primary among these was the sense that school represented a space where children formed significant relationships with teachers and peers, relationships that brought both challenges and opportunities. Relationships with teachers were defined predominantly in terms of learning, the children interspersing their talk with themes of work, the priority teachers gave to some forms of learning over others and the consequent learning environment created in the classroom. While themes of care and concern cut across this talk, in general the children defined their relationships with their teachers in terms of control and regulation, the latter deemed necessary for learning to take place. Such learning challenged the children, sometimes positively and sometimes negatively but on the whole they recognised its significance for their future life chances.

I identified significant differences between groups of children, predominantly to do with age, gender and social class. Younger children and girls appeared more positively disposed to their teachers and their school experience, accepting the level of control and regulation as in their best interests. Boys and older children tended to be more critical, framing their criticisms in terms of resistance to authority and the lack of consultation with children over what they did in school. Social class cut across these dynamics: middle class children were more overtly critical in interviews, yet more visibly compliant in the classroom, while their working class counterparts, particularly a group of older boys in Parkway, were most resistant to the norms of school in their everyday classroom behaviour. Such differences may be explained by the differing affiliation of each social group to the school as an institution, as well as the assertion by the Parkway boys of particular forms of masculinity.

Running parallel with children's relations with teachers were those with their peers. These relationships were defined predominantly in terms of play and the opportunity to escape from the demands of schoolwork and learning. Looking through the lens of child culture revealed the importance of peer relations to the experience of school both in and outside of the classroom. Within the classroom, friends were an important source of support when learning proved too challenging: they provided correct answers, relieved the tedium of lessons through secret games and activities and generally had a laugh, sometimes at the teachers' expense. In the schoolyard, friends provided the impetus for imaginative games and roles and a respite from the relative discipline and order of the classroom. However, the children also faced challenges in their relations with peers that cut across the dimensions of work and play in their experience of school. They were influenced by peer affiliations, so having fun could involve teasing those who were too smart or not smart enough, those who worked hard or did very little, those who were pro or anti school norms. Children's attitudes toward their teachers and their interpretation of curricular, pedagogical and evaluative practices were also influenced by their relations with peers. Their status and inclusion within peer groups were affected by the preferences they expressed.

A second theme that emerged repeatedly in the children's accounts was their absence of control over how their time and space were organised in school. School was experienced as something done to them and over which they exercised little control. This ties in directly with the exercise of power between adults and children in school and, by implication, how childhood is structured through the experience of school.

The exercise of power and the structuring of childhood in school

The analysis provided in Chapter 7 shows that power between adults and children is exercised through the normalisation of children in line with certain ideals. These ideals, expressed through dominant discourses, derive from certain assumptions about children and their learning as well as assumptions about the link between investment in education and national progress and economic development. As adults, teachers are imbued with the authority to exercise control over the time and space of children's school lives, instilling in them the values and skills deemed necessary for their lives as grown ups. That children have no choice but to be at school, to become subject to this power, ensures that the institutionalisation of their lives through schooling is a key characteristic of the structuring of childhood in modern society.

The children's talk was replete with examples of adult power. They remarked on the absence of consultation with them over curricular, pedagogical and evaluative practices in school. Each school was a hive of activity, where teachers and children worked busily to an agenda that emphasised work over play, effort over idleness, obedience over disobedience. Control of this agenda was firmly in adult hands, both at national level through the prescription of the curriculum and at local level in its implementation, as adults decided what and how the children would learn. The very organisation of school space reflected these dynamics of power as the children drew contrasts between the physical resources available to themselves and teachers, as adults, in school. In Foucault's terms the children were being constructed as other, their subordinate status derived from their location within adult discourse as unformed and in need of intervention and control. Children's conformity to school norms, their acceptance of adult control, was predicated on the recognition of the importance of their schoolwork to their future adult lives. In this sense, going to school was perceived as an inevitable fact of life, something that was fully ingrained into the structuring of children's lives. However, the inevitability of schooling is not the same as an unquestioning acceptance of adult control, and for older children especially, fairness in the exercise of adult power was to the forefront of their minds.

While the children perceived teacher power to be relatively absolute, an examination of teacher talk indicated that the teachers themselves felt constrained in carrying out their teaching role. From the teachers' perspectives, the control of children was a necessary prerequisite not only for learning but also for safety and security, partly because of the relatively large groups of children they taught. An important issue that emerged in their talk was the constraint they felt on their practice that derived from this need for crowd control. Thus teachers were constrained by structures that were not of their making: by policy decisions at national level that dictated the level of funding available for investment in primary education and prioritised funding at that level of the education system which ties in more directly with the labour market. The teachers perceived their absence of power as derived primarily from these economic constraints which determine the numbers of pupils in each class and the organisation of pupils for learning. However, teacher practice was also constrained by the very constructions teachers themselves had of children and of their place in the school hierarchy. The emotional investment of teachers in their role, their strong commitment to care for their pupils was framed primarily in terms of child centred discourse. They stressed a nurturing and protective orientation over one which emphasised rights, voice and autonomy for children in school. Teachers also saw their authority as sacrosanct, something to be carefully guarded and at risk from potentially unruly children who, if given a say, might undermine the very status and position of the teachers in the school.

However the research also indicated the capacities of children as agents able to reflect upon and articulate their perceptions of school and the spaces within which they exercised some autonomy and influence over school and classroom processes.

Children and agency in school

As reflective agents, children know what they do and why they do it and this is evident throughout their talk about school. School is a space where children are compulsorily confined; children rationalise such confinement in much the same terms as adults do: that it serves their long term interests for learning that will equip them in their adult lives. They may not agree with the level or nature of their confinement, but on the whole the children acknowledge the importance of having a good education. Children are not cultural dupes, to be moulded unquestioningly in line with adult ideals. As active agents they knowingly participate in the cycle of power in schools – they incorporate definitions of success, learning and achievement into their own worldview and generally conform to the demands of adults for their co-operation and effort in school. The behaviour of those who do not conform also derives from reflected action that denies the significance of schooling to their adult lives. This is based on their assessment of their present lived reality in the broader community.

Children were also shown to be agents through their participation in a shared cultural world of fun and games, where they argued, negotiated and supported one another within a framework of shared rules and understandings. While this social world predominated in the schoolyard, it also permeated the children's experience of classroom life, providing some respite from the demands of learning. Children also exercised agency through the influence they had on their teachers at an interpersonal level, challenging teacher perceptions of what was practicable in their teaching role, requiring teachers to re-evaluate the demands they sometimes made about children's behaviour and learning.

However, what is most notable about children's agency in school is how it is manifested covertly and indirectly. Children exercise influence, not because they are incorporated directly into decision-making about the nature of school life, but through subtly wearing down adult intentions. They do this by working slowly or carelessly, not concentrating, copying, forgetting books/copies, sharpening pencils, engaging the teacher in talk about topics other than the one at hand etc. The children's reliance on these mechanisms stems from their perception that they are not taken seriously as co-participants in school. It also links to their recognition that the teacher is the boss and has the ultimate authority to direct the flow of classroom experience.

The link between discourses of childhood, schooling and education and the formation of children's personal and social identities is central to understanding the structuring of childhood in school. If children are not given a voice and this voice is not heard and listened to, children experience school as imposition: something done by adults to, rather than with, them. The exercise of power is central to this process, translating dominant discourses into practice in an institution characterised by hierarchy, authority and regulation. From an adult view, children's criticisms about school are often not taken seriously but are perceived merely as the inevitable complaints of childhood. However when children's experience is considered in light of the exercise of power between adults and children, these paternalistic assumptions are open to question. There is a fundamental contradiction in a school system that seeks to empower children through education and learning but does not recognise the importance of their voices in that process of empowerment. This is especially pertinent in democratic societies[1]. Furthermore the growing tendency for child/parent relations to be centred on autonomy and negotiation (Whyte, 1995) signals the need for differing patterns of child/adult relations in schools. If children are considered as full members of society we need to start taking them seriously. This is especially important in institutions that are geared toward serving their needs, however the latter may be defined. Such a viewpoint links into discourses related to citizenship and children's rights. It also ties to issues around learning and the empowerment of children through their experiences in school.

Citizenship, rights and learning

The notion of children as citizens who are to be taken seriously as competent actors in society has come to the fore in recent years (Cockburn, 1998; Corsaro, 1997; Devine, 2002; Kjorholt, 2001;

Mayall, 2002; Qvortrup, 1994; Roche, 1999), spurred on by the United Nations Convention on the Rights of the Child (1989). The previous discourse of children's needs is being replaced by a discourse of rights, with implications for children's status in the society as a whole. The publication of the National Children's Strategy (2000) in Ireland signals this changing discourse[2], with its stated vision of:

> An Ireland where children are respected as young citizens with a valued contribution to make and a voice of their own; where all children are cherished and supported by family and the wider society; where they enjoy a fulfilling childhood and realise their potential (Ibid: 4)

This focus on citizenship is also reflected in the school curriculum, where education for citizenship is now seen as an increasingly important aspect of curricular experience at primary and secondary level, mirroring trends elsewhere (Bailey, 2000; Davies, 2001; Kerr *et al*, 2002). However, the trend of education for citizenship does not necessarily imply the empowerment of children through greater recognition of their rights in schools (Devine, 2002). Rather citizenship education in practice can often imply a greater focus on education *about* citizenship rather than furthering the participation and active involvement of children and young people in decision-making in schools. This tension between education about citizenship and the empowerment of children as a specific group is reflected in the Irish Education Act (1998) and recent curricular developments at primary level. In the United Nations Convention on the Rights of the Child (1989), article 27 enshrines students' rights to be informed about the activities of the school and to be actively involved in the operation of the school. At secondary level, students are encouraged to establish a student council. However the requirement for the approval of adult members of the school community (school board) sets clear conditions for the enactment of student rights in this area. The failure to consider student councils in primary schools indicates that the capacities of this age group to involve themselves more directly in the schooling process are underestimated, as evidenced in recent research in this area (McLoughlin, 2002). The Revised Primary Curriculum of Ireland (1999), also signals some important advances. It notes the significance of children's active involvement in decision-making in the development of citizenship (through the SPHE programme) but it stops short of identifying locales within the school where children can actively exercise their voice.

This tension brings us directly to the exercise of power between adults and children and how learning is defined and experienced in schools. The work of Vygotsky (1978 and 1991) indicates how learning is intertwined with the dynamics of power and control between children and adults, pupils and teachers in two ways. Firstly the influence of the broader socio-cultural context provides the definition and understanding of what is considered important in children's socialisation[3]. This links in with the analysis in Chapter 7 on the discourses of childhood and schooling in modern society. Such discourses form part of the cultural and social context within which child/adult, pupil/teacher relations are constructed and comprise one aspect of the social plane on which learning is based. Secondly, the exercise of power is implicit in Vygotsky's concept of scaffolding – whereby the child is supported and guided by adults through the zone of proximal development. Vygotsky shows how the adult can encourage the child to independence when a relationship of trust, dialogue and understanding is developed. Where the child/ adult relationship is characterised by hierarchy and control a less effective form of learning takes place. Other research indicates how children's movement through the zone of proximal development is influenced by the extent to which they are encouraged to take risks and are shown respect and tolerance in their relations with teachers (Pollard, 1996; Pollard and Triggs, 2001). The growing movement of philosophy with children is also indicative of the critical capacities of children and how actively involving children in their own learning can foster higher order thinking (Donnelly, 2001).

Thus discourse related to children's rights and citizenship accords with discourse on children's learning and development. Involving children as co-participants in the organisation of school life can be framed not only in terms of a rights perspective (as articulated in the United Nations Convention on the Rights of the Child 1989), but also in terms of scaffolding their learning by establishing a school environment which challenges and extends children's (as well as adults') development through tolerance, respect and dialogue. This can take place at the level of classroom practice – in the implementation of the curriculum as well as in the patterns of pupil/teacher relations within the classroom – and at school level by directly involving children in decisions about school life. Research into the operation of student councils on a genuine (rather than token) basis of openness highlights the positive impact for children as they grapple with the challenges and opportunities posed by an increased voice in school affairs (Klein, 2003; McLoughlin, 2002; Jelly *et al* 2000; Willow, 1990).

Discourse related to children's rights and citizenship needs to be incorporated into discourse on schooling, shaping children's identities and being shaped by children's identity, so facilitating their participation as social actors in the cycle of power in schools. Agency is conceived in terms of children's capacities to resist adult control as well as their capacities to transform aspects of school practice through exercising their voice on matters of concern to them[4]. The concept of children's citizenship is a central guiding principle in the organisation of school life. It should inform all aspects of practice, rather than being isolated as a subject to be learned, divorced from the lived realities of teachers' and pupils' experience. The theoretical analysis presented in Chapter 7 would illustrate the experience of schooling thus:

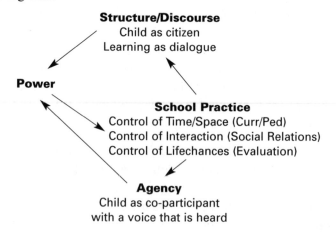

Figure 2: Citizenship, power and the structuring of childhood in school

Achieving a more democratic experience of school for children will not succeed in practice unless teachers, as adults, are convinced of the merits of incorporating children's voices into the running and organisation of schools. Children *have* rights to greater active involvement and information on matters affecting them, and the incorporation of these rights, although minimal, into legislation signifies an important advance in children's position in schools. However there is a danger that in the absence of teacher training and critical reflection in this area such legislative provisions will generate only token practice on the ground and there will be little change in the prevailing dynamics of power and control in schools. Critical reflection and training for teachers on this subject will require them to question the paternalistic assumptions they themselves may hold about children's capacities to contribute constructively to the organisation of a school. Teachers will need to rethink their concept of power as solely a matter of authority and control and instead examine how power is exercised between adults and children. The benefits for adults and children alike of listening to children need to be explored, particularly with reference to the impact on children's learning and development.

The move toward involving children more directly in school life requires teachers to take a certain amount of risk as they open themselves to more dialogical relations with their pupils. Research has shown how this can bring with it both challenges and opportunities for the teachers and pupils involved (Anderson, 2000; Jelly *et al*, 2000, McLoughlin 2002, Roche, 1999; Wyness, 2000). The culture of the school provides the context within which new strategies for improving practice are worked through and explored. If this culture is characterised by support, dynamism and an openness to change then initiatives related to the active inclusion of children in school affairs are likely to be more successful. Such cultures in themselves will tend to be more democratic and less hierarchical than those characterised by an unwillingness to change and rooted in the status quo (Hargreaves, 1995; Swan and Devine, 2002; Teddlie and Reynolds, 2001). We have seen throughout this book how children's perspectives can differ from, as well as converge with those of adults. The challenge lies with incorporating and taking children's views and perspectives seriously and relating them to practice in schools.

Feeling valued, respected and heard is an important element in school culture and the gains brought to school life when teachers and parents feel heard and listened to will be more than matched when children are treated in a similar way.

Extending children's role as active participants in school

What does the greater involvement of children in school affairs entail? Returning to our model, at the level of discourse it means recognising the position of children as competent actors with the right, as citizens, to have their voices heard in all matters affecting them in school. Underpinning this is the notion of learning as dialogue: to critically engage with children about all aspects of their experience is a valuable aspect of their education. This has implications for practice at national, school and class levels.

At national level it means incorporating the views of children in the development of policy, as for example in the consultative process undertaken with children as part of the development of the National Children's Strategy in Ireland (2000). Steps are currently underway to increase the active participation by children generally by establishing a children's parliament (Dáil Na NÓg) and appointing an ombudsman for children. Though this is just a beginning, these steps signal the greater attention being given by state bodies to the rights and voice of children, in line with the United Nations Convention on the Rights of the Child (1989)[5]. To date there has been little structured consultation involving children in the educational sphere. Partnership in education is defined primarily in adult centred terms as including parents, teachers, State Department officials and Patron Bodies (Devine, 2001). Although there is evidence of an increasing awareness of incorporating the voices of second level students[6] in research based policy development (e.g. Govt of Ireland, 1998; NCCA, 2003) consultation with children at primary level has been markedly lacking.

At school level, incorporating children's voices can take a number of forms. The Education Act in Ireland (1998) affords student councils some status in terms of accessing children's voices. Research indicates how useful such councils can be as a forum for listening to children's views (McLoughlin, 2002; Jelly *et al*, 2000). It also highlights how school practice can be positively transformed by taking account of the voices of children and how they, like adults, learn important lessons about responsibility, patience, leadership and listening to others.

The importance of preparing children for committee membership has also been noted in research (Danielsen, 1989; McLoughlin, 2002; Smit, 1989). Preparation not only signals the seriousness with which the enterprise of a student council is taken but it also equips children with the skills to articulate their views, conduct meetings and actively contribute to the workings of the council. The relationship between the student council and school board and the representation of the voice of students at Board level is also important. It can take a number of forms, such as having a student member directly represented on the board or having a students' advocate who is familiar with the deliberations of the student council. Participation in a council can take many forms adapted to suit the age and requirements of the participants. Induction into participation in a student council can take place gradually. From the time they enter primary school, children can be encouraged to develop skills in democratic participation that will facilitate their capacities to actively engage in council membership. There is a fundamental link between the pedagogical practice at class level and the school level policies geared toward the greater active involvement of children in school affairs. The success of a student council should not be conditional upon an adult member of staff having the interest and motivation to make the council work. If a student council is perceived as an integral aspect of the functioning of the school (as is for example the School Board) then due recognition should be given to it by structuring teacher professional responsibilities accordingly (through for example an assigned post of responsibility) in schools.

Whole School Planning designed for school improvement can be used as a vehicle for inviting and incorporating the voices of children in the vision for a school. One area where children are often part of school planning is that of the development of disciplinary and anti-bullying strategies. This gives children some sense of ownership over regulatory mechanisms in the school. But their involvement in school planning should not be confined to the disciplinary field alone. As a first step in consultation it can be useful, however, giving children a sense of ownership over an aspect of school experience about which they can have strong views. But involvement should not stop there. Peer support networks and advocacy systems have also been identified as useful mechanisms within which children can be facilitated to become more actively involved in managing their behaviour in schools (Wyness, 1999:363).

What takes place at school level should correspond to and be supported by practice at class level. There are proven strategies of inclusion for listening to the voices of children at class level such as workshop education, co-operative learning and circle time. A climate of inclusion of children's voices can be promoted by involving them actively in decisions related to the organisation of their time and space in the classroom. This means teasing through with them their perception of the curricular, pedagogical and evaluative practices in the classroom, inviting them as co-participants to constructively evaluate and contribute to the learning environment in *their* (as opposed to the teachers') classroom. The issues that emerge will vary from year to year and class to class, but will typically involve maintaining a balance between the need for learning and the desire for fun in a context that is safe and secure for all members of the class.

Concluding remarks

The voices of children conveyed in this book indicate that what children want most from their schooling is to be taught clearly, to be treated fairly and to be taken seriously by adults in school. The authority of teachers is not in itself called into question. Children recognise and generally support teachers' position of authority in schools. What children ask for is that this position be used to construct an experience of school that is engaging and meaningful, that supports the learning the children need for their adult lives in a manner that also acknowledges their priorities as children.

How much are children's complaints about school an inevitable feature of childhood? Are they an outcome of the way in which schools are structured around goals and values which have their origins in the adult world of work and productivity and not in the child's world? In the daily exercise of power between adults and children how do we, as adults, define the purpose of education? And how do we value the experiences and conditions of children's lives? My analysis of the exercise of power between adults and children has shown the importance of economic and authoritative resources in the translation into practice of discourses about children and childhood. One measure of children's status in society is the level of investment that is made, in the provision of services for children. By this measure, investment in Irish primary education falls short of what is required. This has direct implications for how children's experience of school is structured – in terms of class size and the provision of schools that are well resourced and functionally equipped to facilitate the implementation of an activity based curriculum.

This is replicated across the developed world. How teachers exercise the power they have in schools has real consequences not only for children's experience but also for their sense of themselves as persons with a voice to be heard. If we challenge the stereotypes of children as immature and socially incompetent, the authoritative position of teachers can be harnessed to support children's learning in a more democratic manner. While this poses challenges for the teachers in terms of their own perceptions of power and control, it is worth taking the risk. Failing to take this risk is to perpetuate a cycle of power that constructs children as other and is increasingly removed from the broader changing context of children's lives.

Notes

1 There is a substantial literature on the link between democracy and schooling. See for example the classic work of Dewey (1963), Freire (1972) and more recent work by Apple and Benne (1999), Giroux (1989), Gutman (1999), Hahn (1999), Kerr *et al* (2002), Osler and Starkey (2002), Print *et al* (2002).

2 As the first document of its kind the National Children's Strategy 2000 is a welcome development in Irish society. However it has not been immune to criticism (e.g Deegan, 2002, Devine, Nic Ghiolla Phádraig and Deegan, 2003) and concerns have been expressed over the translation of the rhetoric into practice as in for example the delayed appointment of an ombudsman for children.

3 This obviously varies from one cultural context to another. For our purposes, however, a key element of children's socialisation in western democracies is their compulsory attendance at school. Schools, with all their cultural meanings and definitions of legitimate practice, are a key element of the social plane defined by Vygotsky (1978 and 1991) as so essential to children's development.

4 The extent to which children can actually transform what happens in school will vary by the context being considered. A curriculum prescribed at national level places constraints on both teachers and pupils over what is taught and learned in schools. Curricular priorities in turn affect the evaluative systems used in schools, with teachers, particularly toward the senior end of the primary school often feeling compelled to reinforce learning in the core areas of mathematics and language by persistently evaluating children in these areas. The study showed that children exercised very little agency in each of these areas. However there appears to be greater potential for children's agency, hence transformative capacity in the pedagogical and social relations field. This was borne out in the differing styles and personalities of teachers which evoked differing learning climates in each class, and in the teachers' comments on how they had changed their practice in light of children's responses.

5 The slow pace of change in relation to these measures, as in for example not appointing an Ombudsman, has given rise to some criticism and concerns over the government's real commitment to implementing in practice the rhetoric of the National Children's Strategy (CRA, 2003).

6 Second level students are themselves becoming increasingly aware of the need to articulate their voice on educational policy generally. This is evident in the recent establishment of the Union of Secondary Students in Ireland in response to concerns that student views as stakeholders were not being taken into account in a protracted dispute between second level teachers and the Government over pay and work conditions.

References

Alanen, L and Mayall, B (2001) *Conceptualising Child-Adult Relations*, London, Routledge Falmer

Aldeerson, P (2000) *Children's Rights and School Councils, Children and Society*, 121-134, London, John Wiley and Sons

Althusseur, L (1972) Ideology and Ideological State Apparatuses (Notes towards an investigation) in Cosin, B (ed) *Education, Structure and Society*, Harmondsworth, Penguin

Anyon, J (1981) Social Class and School Knowledge in *Curriculum Inquiry*, 11:1, 3-42

Anyon, J (1981) Elementary Schooling and Distinctions of Social Class, *Educational Policy*, Vol 12, No 2-3, 118-132

Apple, M (1979) *Ideology and Curriculum*, London, Routledge and Kegan Paul

Apple, M (1982) *Education and Power*, New York, Routledge and Kegan Paul

Apple, M (1982) *Cultural and Economic Reproduction in Education*, London, Routledge and Kegan Paul

Apple, M (1986) *Teachers and Text*, New York, Routledge and Kegan Paul

Apple, M and Benne, J (eds) (1999) Democratic Schools: Lessons from the Chalk Face, Buckingham, Open University Press

Apple, M (2002) Does Education have Independent Power? Bernstein and the question of Relative Autonomy, *British Journal of Sociology of Education*, Vol 23, No 4: 607-616

Archard, D (1993) *Children, Rights and Childhood*, London, Routledge

Archer, M (1979) *Social Origins of Educational Systems*, London, Sage

Archer, M (1990) Human Agency and Social Structure: A critique of Giddens in Clark J (ed) *Anthony Giddens – Consensus and Controversy*, London, Falmer Press

Archer, M (1998) Social Theory and the Analysis of Society, in May, T and Williams, M (eds) *Knowing the Social World*, Buckingham, Open University Press

Bailey, R (2000) *Teaching Values and Citizenship Across the Curriculum*, London, Kogan Page

Barker, P (1998) *Michel Foucault: An Introduction*, Edinburgh, Edinburgh University Press

Barnett, Y (1988) 'Miss, girls don't like playing big games; they only like playing little games': gender differences in the use of playground space, *Primary Teaching Studies*, 4: 1, 42-52

Bennett deMarrais, K and LeCompte, M.D (1999) *The Way Schools Work: a Sociological Analysis of Education*, New York, Longman

Benson, C (2001) *The Cultural Psychology of Self*, London, Routledge

Bernstein, B (1996) *Pedagogy, Symbolic Control and Identity: Theory, Research, Critique,* London, Taylor Francis

Bernstein, B (1975) *Class, Codes and Control: Towards a theory of Educational Transmission* (Vol 3), London, Routledge and Kegan Paul

Bernstein, B (1990) *The Structure of Pedagogic Discourse,* London, Routledge Falmer

Blatchford, P (1989) *Playtime in the Primary School: Problems and Improvements,* Windsor, NFER

Blatchford, P and Cresser, R (1991) Playground Games and Playground Time: the children's view in Woodhead, M and Light, P (eds): *Growing up in a Changing Society,* London, Routledge

Blatchford, S (1996) *Social Life in School: Pupils' Experience of Breaktime and Recess from 7-16 years,* London, Falmer

Blitzer, S (1991) 'They are only children, what do they know?' A look at current ideologies of children, Adler, P (ed) *Sociological Studies of Child Development,* Vol 4, 11.

Bloomer, M (2001) 'Young Lives, Learning and Transformation: some theoretical considerations'; *Oxford Review of Education,* Vol 27, No 3, 429-449

Blyth, E and Milner, J (1993) 'Exclusion from school: A first step in exclusion from society?' *Children and Society,* 7 (3) 255-268

Bodine, A (2003) School uniforms and discourses on childhood, *Childhood,* Vol 10, No 1 43-65

Bourdieu, P (1993) *The Field of Cultural Production,* London, Sage

Bourdieu, P (1996) *The State Nobility – Elite Schools in the Field of Power,* Oxford, Polity Press

Bourdieu, P and Passeron, J. C (1977) *Reproduction in Education, Society and Culture,* London, Sage

Bourne, J (2001) Discourses and Identities in a Multi-Lingual Primary Classroom, in *Oxford Review of Education,* Vol 27, No 1: 113 – 114

Bowles, S and Gintis, H (1976) *Schooling in Capitalist America,* London, Routledge and Kegan Paul

Brennan, M (2000) *Teacher's Perspectives on the Child's Right to be Heard,* Unpublished M.Ed thesis, Education Dept, University College Dublin

Broadfoot, P (1996) *Education: Assessment and Society,* Buckingham: Open University Press

Brown, P and Lauder, H (1996) Education, Globalisation and Economic Development, *Journal of Education Policy,* 1: 1-24

Bruner, J (1996) *The Culture of Education,* Cambridge, Harvard University Press

Butler, I and Shaw, I (1996) *A Case of Neglect: Children's Experiences and the Sociology of Childhood,* Aldershot, Avebury

Campbell, J (1998) Primary Teaching: Roles and relationships, in Richards, C and Taylor, P (eds) *How Shall We School Our Children? Primary Education and its Future,* London, Falmer

Christensen, P and James, A (2001) What are schools for? The temporal experience of children's learning in northern England, Alanen, L and Mayall, B (eds) *Conceptualising Child-Adult Relations,* London, Falmer

Cleary, A, Nic Ghiolla Phadraig, M and Quin, S (2001) (eds) *Understanding Children,* Volume 1 and 2, Dublin, Oak Tree Press

Cockburn, T (1998) 'Children and Citizenship in Britain', *Childhood* 5 (1):99-117

Coffey, A (2001) *Education and Social Change,* Buckingham, Open University Press

Coleman, J (1998) 'Social Capital in the Creation of Human Capital', *American Journal of Sociology,* 94: S95-S120

Cooley, C (1902) *Human Nature and the Social Order,* New York, Scribner

Collins, J (2000) 'Are you talking to me?' The need to respect and develop a pupil's self image in *Educational Research* 42: 2 ; 157-166

Connell, R (1995) *Masculinities*, Cambridge, Polity Press

Connolly, P (1998) *Racism, Gender Identities and Young Children*, London, Routledge

Conway, P (2002) Learning in Communities of Practice: Rethinking Teaching and Learning in Disadvantaged Contexts in *Irish Educational Studies*, 21 (3) : 61-93

Corsaro, W. A (1997) *The Sociology of Childhood*, London: Pine Forge Press

Cousins, M and Hussain, A (1984) *Michel Foucault*, London, MacMillan

Craib, I (1992) *Anthony Giddens,* London, Routledge

Crocker, T and Cheeseman, R (1991) 'The ability of young children to rank themselves for academic ability' in Woodhead, M, Light, P and Carr, R (eds) *Growing up in a Changing Society*, London, Routledge/Open University Press

Cullingford, C (1991) *The Inner World of the School: Children's ideas about Schools,* London, Cassell

Danielson, N (1989) Helping pupils to help themselves: Pupils' Councils and Participation, Jensen, K and Walker, S (eds) *Towards Democratic Schooling*, Milton Keynes, Open University Press

Darmarin, M (1995) Classroom practices and class pedagogies, in J Salisbury and S Delamont (eds) *Qualitative Studies in Education*, London: Avebury

Davies, B (1982) *Life in the Classroom and Playground. The Accounts of Primary School Children*, London, Routledge and Kegan Paul

Davies, B (1983) The role pupils play in the social construction of classroom order, *British Journal of Sociology of Education*, 4 (1) 55-69

Davies, B (1990) Agency as a form of Discursive Practice, A Classroom Scene Observed, in *British Journal of Sociology of Education*, Vol 11, No 3, 1990: 341-361

Davies, B (1991) Friends and Fights, in Woodhead, M and Light, P (eds) *Growing up in Changing Society*, London, Routledge

Davies, L (2001) 'Citizenship, Education and Contradiction', *British Journal of Sociology of Education*, 22 (2): 300-308

Deegan, J (2002) Early Childhood Discourse: Problematising Some Conceptual Issues in Statutory Frameworks, *Irish Educational Studies*, Vol 21, No 3: 77-88

Department of Education (1990) *Report of the Primary Review Body on the Primary Curriculum*, Dublin, Mount Salus Press

Devine, D (1991) A Study of Reading Ability Groups: Primary School Children's Experiences and Views in *Irish Educational Studies*, Vol 12: 134-143

Devine, D (1999) Children: Rights and Status in Education – a Socio historical Perspective, *Irish Educational Studies*, 18:14-29

Devine, D (2000) Constructions of Childhood in School: power, policy and practice in Irish education, *International Studies in Sociology of Education*, Vol 10, Number 1:23-41

Devine, D (2002) Children's Citizenship and the structuring of adult-child relations in the primary school, *Childhood,* Vol 9(3) 303-321

Devine, D and Kenny, M with MacNeela, E (2002) *Ethnicity and Schooling: A study of ethnic diversity in a selected sample of Irish primary and post-primary schools*, Education Dept, National University of Ireland, Dublin

Devine, D, Nic Ghiolla Phádraig, M and Deegan, J (forthcoming) *Country Report Ireland: COST Action '19': Children's Welfare*, Dept of Sociology and Dept of Education, National University Ireland, Dublin

Dewey, J (1963) *Experience and Education*, London, Collier-MacMillan

Donnelly, P (2001) 'A Study of Higher Order Thinking, the Early Years Classroom through doing Philosophy, *Irish Educational Studies*, Vol 20, 278-295

Drudy, S and Lynch, K (1993) *Schools and Society in Ireland*, Dublin, Gill and MacMillan

Drudy, S and Ui Chatháin, M (1999) *Gender Equality in Classroom Interaction*, Maynooth Education Dept, National University of Ireland Maynooth

Durkheim, E (1956) *Education and Society*, New York, Free Press

Durkheim, E (1964) *The Division of Labour in Society,* New York, Free Press

Elliot, J, Hufton, N, Illushin, L and Fraser, L (2001) Motivation in the Junior Years: international perspectives on children's attitudes, expectations and behaviour and their relationship to educational achievement in *Oxford Review of Education*, vol 27, No 1: 37-68

Entwistle, N (1974) *Child Centred Education,* London, Methuen

Ferriter, D (2002) Suffer little children? The Historical Validity of Memoirs of Irish Childhood in Dunne, J and Kelly, J (eds) *Childhood and its Discontents*, Dublin, Liffey Press

Filer, A and Pollard, A (2000) *The Social World of Pupil Assessment,* London, Continuum

Foucault, M (1979a) *Discipline and Punish: the Birth of the Prison*, New York, Random House

Foucault, M (1979b) *The History of Sexuality*, Volume 1, London, Allen Lane

Foucault, M (1980) *Michel Foucault: Power Knowledge*, Hertfordshire, Harvester Wheatsheaf

Foucault, M (1982) The Subject and Power in Dreyfus, H and Rabinow, P: Michel Foucault – *Beyond Structuralism and Hermeneutics*, Chicago, Chicago University Press

Francis, B (1998) *Power Plays: Children's Construction of Gender, Power and Adult Work*, Stoke-on-Trent, Trentham Books

Franklin, B (1986) *The Rights of Children*, Oxford, Blackwell

Freire, P (1972) *Pedagogy of the Oppressed*, New York, Penguin

Galton, M, Hargreaves, L, Comber, C, Wall, D and Pell, A (1999) *Inside the Primary Classroom: 20 years on*, London, Routledge

Gardner, H (1993) *Multiple Intelligences: the Theory in Practice*, New York, Basis Books

Gardner, H (1997) *Leading Minds: an Anatomy of Leadership*, London, Harper Collins

Gardner, H (1999) *Intelligence Reframed: Multiple Intelligences for the 21st century*, New York, Basis Books

Giddens, A (1979) *Central Problems in Social Theory: Action, Structure and Contradiction in Social Analysis*, London, MacMillan

Giddens, A (1984) *The Constitution of Society – Outline of the Theory of Structuration*, Los Angeles, University of California Press

Giroux, H (1989) *Schooling for Democracy,* London, Routledge and Kegan Paul

Goffman, E (1961) *Asylums*, Chicago, Aldine Publishing Company

Goffman, E (1971) *The Presentation of Self in Everyday Life*, London, Penguin

Goodnow, J and Burns, A (1985) *Home and School – A Child's Eye View*, London, Allen and Unwin

Goodnow, J and Burns, A (1991) Teachers; a Child's Eye View in Woodhead, M, Light, P and Carr, R (eds) *Growing up in a Changing Society,* London, Routledge

Government of Ireland (2000) *The National Children's Strategy*, Dublin, Stationery Office

Government of Ireland (1999) *Revised Primary Curriculum*, Dublin, The Stationery Office

Government of Ireland (1998) Education Act

Grugeon, E (1993) Gender in the Playground in Woods, P and Hammersly, M (eds) *Gender and Ethnicity,* Buckingham, Open University Press

Gutman, A (1999) *Democratic Education,* Princeton, Princeton University Press

Hahn, C (1999) Citizenship Education: an empirical study of policy, practices and outcomes, *Oxford Review of Education*, Vol 25, No1 /2, 231-250

Hammersly, M and Woods, P (eds) (1984) *Life in School: the Sociology of Pupil Culture,* Minton Keynes, Open University Press

Hargreaves, A (1994) *Changing Teachers, Changing Times*, London, Cassell

Hargreaves, A (2000) 'Mixed emotions: teacher's perceptions of their interactions with students' *Teaching and Teacher Education*, 16: 811-826

Hargreaves, D (1995) School Culture, School Effectiveness and School Improvement, in *School Effectiveness and School Improvement*, Vol 6, No 1: 23-46

Harré, R (1993) *Social Being*, Oxford, Blackwell

Haste, H (1987) Growing into Rules, in Haste, J and Bruner, J (eds) *Making Sense,* London, Methuen

Hartley, D (2003) New Economy, New Pedagogy? in *Oxford Review of Education*,Vol 29, No 1: 81-94

Hayes, N and McKernan, M (2001) *Seven Years Old: School Experience in Ireland*, National Report of the IEA Preprimary Project 3, Dublin, Dublin Institute of Technology

Hendrick, H (1997) Constructions and Reconstructions of British Childhood: An Interpretative Study 1800 to the present, in James, A, Prout, and Jencks, C (eds) *Constructing and Reconstructing Childhood: Contemporary Issues in the Sociological Study of Childhood*, London, Falmer

INTO (1985) *Primary School Curriculum – Report and Discussion Papers,* Dublin, INTO

Jackson, P (1968) *Life in Classrooms*, Chicago, Holt, Rinehart and Winston

James, C (1998) From the Child's Point of View: Issues in the Social Construction of Childhood, in Panter-Brick, C (ed) (1998) *Biosocial Perspectives on Children*, Cambridge, University Press

James, C, Jenks, C and Prout, A (1998) *Theorising Childhood*, London, Polity

James, A and Prout, A (1997) *Constructing and Reconstructing Childhood: Contemporary Issues in the Sociological Study of Childhood*, London, Falmer

Jelly M, Fuller, A and Byers, R (2000) *Involving Pupils in Practice*, Wilts: Cromwell Press

Jenks, C (1996) *Childhood*, London, Routledge

Kerr, D; McCarthy, S and Smith, A (2002) 'Citizenship Education in England, Ireland and Northern Ireland, *European Journal of Education*, Vol 37:No 2:179-191

King, R (1989) *The Best of Primary Education? A Sociological Study of Junior Middle Schools*, London, Falmer

King, R (1978) *All Things Bright and Beautiful? A Sociological Study of Infants' Classrooms,* New York, John Wiley and Sons

Kjorholt, A.T (2001) 'The Participating Child' A Vital Pillar in this century? *Nordisk Pedagogik*, Vol 21, 65-81

Klein, R (2003) *We want our say – children as active participants in their education*, Stoke on Trent, Trentham

Layder, D (1994) *Understanding Social Theory*, London, Sage

Layder, D (1997) *Modern Social Theory: Key Debates and New Directions*, London, UCL Press

Leach, J and Moon, B (Eds) (1999) *Learners and Pedagogy*, London, Paul Chapman

Levine, R (1998) Child Psychology and Anthropology: an environmental view, in Panter-Brick, C (ed) (1998) *Biosocial Perspectives on Children,* Cambridge, Cambridge University Press

Lodge, A and Flynn, M (2001) Gender Identity in the Primary School Playground in Cleary, A, NicGhiolla Phádraig, M and Quin, S (eds) *Understanding Children*, Volume 2, Dublin, Oak Tree Press

Lortie, D (1975) *School Teacher – A Sociological Study*, University of Chicago

Lynch, K (1989) *The Hidden Curriculum: Reproduction in Education: A Reappraisal*, Lewes, Falmer Press

Lynch, K and Lodge, A (2002) *Equality and Power in Schools: Redistribution, Recognition and Representation*, London, Routledge Falmer

Mac an Ghaill, M (1994) *The Making of Men: Masculinities, Sexualities and Schooling*, Buckingham, Open University Press

Mac an Ghaill, M (1999) *Contemporary Racisms and Ethnicities, Social and Cultural Transformations,* Buckingham, Open University Press

MacRuairc, G (1977) 'Big Mad Words', Perceptions of Language Variation in Schools: A Sociological Analysis, Unpublished M.Ed Thesis, Education Dept, National University of Ireland, Dublin

McLouglin, O (2002) Citizen Child: A Case Study of a Student Council in a Primary School, Unpublished M.Ed thesis, Education Dept, National University of Ireland, Dublin

McNay, L (1994) *Foucault: A Critical Introduction*, London, Polity Press

Manke, M (1994) *Teacher Organisation of Time and Space in the Classroom as an aspect of Classroom Power Relationships*, Paper presented at the AERA annual meeting New Orleans, April 1994

Mayall, B (1994) *Children's Childhoods Observed and Experienced,* London, Falmer

Mayall, B (1996) *Children, Health and Social Order,* Buckingham, Open University Press

Mayall, B (2002) *Towards a Sociology for Childhood*, Buckingham, Open University Press

Mead, G.H (1972) *Mind, Self and Society*, London, University of Chicago Press

McCallum, B, Hargreaves, E and Gipps, C (2000) 'Learning: the pupils' voice', *Cambridge Journal of Education*, 30, Vol 2

Means, B; Chelemer, C; Knapp, M.S. (eds) (1991) *Teaching Advanced Skills to At-risk Students: Views from Research and Practice,* San Francisco: Jossey-Bass Inc; Publishers

Montondon, C and Osiek, F (1998) Children's Perspectives on their Education, *Childhood*, Vol 5 (3):247-263

Moore, G and Lackney, J (1993) 'School Design: Crisis, Educational Performance and Design Applications, *Children's Environments*, 10 (2): 99-112

Morrow, V (1995) 'Invisible Children? Toward a reconceptualisation of Childhood Dependency and Responsibility, Mandell, N (eds): *Sociological Studies of Children*, Vol 7

Morrow, V and Richards, M (1996) The Ethics of Social Research with Children: An Overview, *Children and Society*, Vol 10 No 2: 90-105

NCCA (1990) *Report of the Review Body on the Primary Curriculum*, Dept of Education, Dublin, The Stationery Office

NCCA (2003) Developing the Senior Cycle – Education on line survey, www.ncca.ie

Nias, J (1989) *Primary Teachers Talking*, London, Routledge

Nic Ghiolla Phadraig, M (2001) 'Tá Gaeilge agam ach ní ag mo chara' Irish speaking Children in Cleary, A, Nic Ghiolla Phádraig, M and Quinn, S (eds) *Understanding Children*, Volume 2, Dublin, Oak Tree Press

Oakes, J (1985) *Keeping Track: How Schools Structure Inequality,* London, Yale University Press

Oakes, J and Lipton, M (1999) *Teaching to Change the World,* Boston, McGraw College

O'Moore, M, Kirkham, C and Smith, M (1997) Bullying Behaviour in Irish Schools: A nation-wide study, *Irish Journal of Psychology,* 18 (2) 141-169

O'Moore, M and Minton, S (2003) The Hidden Voice of Bullying in Shevlin, M and Rose, (eds) *Encouraging Voices: respecting the rights of young people who have been marginalized,* Dublin, National Disability Authority

Opie, I and Opie, P (1991) The Culture of Children in Waksler, F (ed) *Studying the Social Worlds of Children,* London, Falmer Press

Opie, I (1994) *The People in the Playground,* Oxford, Oxford University Press

Osborn, M, McNess, E and Broadfoot, P with Pollard, A and Triggs, P (2000) *What Teachers Do: Changing Policy and Practice in Primary Education,* London, Cassell

Osler, A and Starkey, H (2002) Education for Citizenship: Mainstreaming the fight against racism?; *European Journal of Education,* Vol 27, No 2:143-159

O'Sullivan, D (1979) Negotiation in the Maintenance of Social Control: A Study in an Irish Correctional School in *International Journal of Criminology and Penology,* Vol 6 31-42

O'Sullivan, D (1980) Teacher Socialisation and Teaching Style in an Irish Cultural Context, *European Journal of Education,* Vol 15, No 4

O'Sullivan, D (1984) Social Class and Sexual Variations in Teachers' Perceptions of their Pupils, *Oideas,* Vol 28, 15-24

Paetcher, C (1998) *Educating the Other: Gender, Power and Schooling,* London, Falmer Press

Panter-Brick, C (ed) (1998) *Biosocial Perspectives on Children,* Cambridge, University Press

Parsons, T (1951) *The Social System,* London, Routledge

Parons, T (1964) *Social Structure and Personality,* New York, Free Press

Peters, M (202) 'Truth telling as an Educational Practice of the Self: Foucault, Parrhesia and the Ethics of Subjectivity, in *Oxford Review of Education,* Vol 29, No 2, 207-223

Pollard, A (1985) *The Social World of the Primary School,* Guilford, Biddles

Pollard, A (1987) *Children and their Primary Schools,* London, Falmer

Pollard, A (1990) Towards a Sociology of Learning in Primary Schools, *British Journal of Sociology of Education,* Vol 11, No 3, 241 -256

Pollard, A (1996) *The Social World of Children's Learning,* London, Cassell

Pollard, A and Filer, A (1996) *The Social World of Children's Learning: Case Studies of Pupils from four to Seven,* London, Cassell

Pollard, A, and Filer, A (1999) *The Social World of Pupil Career: Strategic Biographies Through Primary School,* London, Cassell

Pollard, A, Thiessen, D and Filer, A (eds) (1997) *Children and their Curriculum: The Perspectives of Primary and Elementary School Children,* London, Falmer

Pollard, A and Triggs,, P (2000) *What Pupils Say: Changing Policy and Practice in Primary Education,* London, Continuum

Postman, N (1994) *The Disappearance of Childhood,* London, Allen

Print, M, Ornstrom. S and Skovgaard Neilsen, H (2002) Education for Democratic Processes in Schools and Classrooms, *European Journal of Education,* Vol 37: 2:193-210

Qvortrup, J (1987) *Introduction to Thematic Issues on the Sociology of Childhood,* Vienna, European Centre for Social Welfare Policy and Research

Ovortrup, J (1994) Childhood Matters: an introduction in Qvortrup, J, Bardy, M, Sgritta, G and Wintersberger, H (eds) *Childhood Matters: Social Theory, Practice and Politics,* Aldershot, Avebury

Qvortrup, J (2001) Schoolwork, Paidwork and the changing obligations of childhood in Mizen, P, Pole, C and Bolton, A (eds) *Hidden Hands: International Perspectives on Children's work and Labour,* London, Routledge Falmer

Reay, D and William, D (1999) 'I'll be a nothing' – structure, agency and the construction of identity through assessment, *British Education Research Journal*, 25 (3) 343-354

Roche, J (1999) Children: Rights, Participation and Citizenship, *Childhood* 6(4): 475-93

Sampson, R, Morenoff, J and Earls, F (1999) Beyond social capital: spatial dynamics of collective efficacy for children, in *American Sociological Review*, Vol 64, 633-666

Schilling, C (1992) Reconceptualising Structure and Agency in the Sociology of Education: structuration theory and schooling, *British Journal of Sociology of Education*, Vol 134, No 1, 69-87

Sharp, R and Green, A (1975) *Education and Social Control*, London, Routledge and Kegan Paul

Singh, P (2002) Pedagogising Knowledge: Bernstein's theory of the Pedagogic Device, *British Journal of Sociology of Education*, Vol 23, No 4: 571-582

Sluckin, A (1981) *Growing up in the Playground*, London, Routledge and Kegan Paul

Smit, F (1989) 'The need for a pupil's statute in a Democratic School' Jensen, K and Walker, S (eds) *Towards Democratic Schooling*, Milton Keynes, Open University Press

Smyth, E (1999) *Do Schools Differ? Academic and Personal Development among Pupils in the second level sector*, Dublin, Oak Tree

Spencer, S (2000) The Implications of the Human Rights Act for Citizenship Education, in Osler, A *Citizenship and Democracy in Schools: Diversity, Identity and Equality,* 19-32 Stoke on Trent, Trentham Books

Sternberg, R . J (1998) 'How intelligent is intelligence testing' in *Scientific American*, 9 , 4 12-17

Sternber, R. J (2002) *Cognitive Psychology,* London, Wadsworth

Sugrue, C (1997) *Complexities of Teaching: Child Centred Perspectives*, London, Falmer

Swan, D and Devine, D (2002) Case Studies of more effective and less effective schools in the Republic of Ireland, in Reynolds D, Creemers B, Stringfield S, Teddlie C and Schaffer, G (eds) *World Class Schools: International Perspectives on School Effectiveness,* London, Routledge Falmer

Teddlie, C and Reynolds, D (2001) *International Handbook of School Effectiveness and Improvement,* London, Falmer

Thorne, B (1993) *Gender Play: Girls and Boys in School*, Buckingham, Open University Press

Tirri, K and Poulinatha, J (2000) 'Teacher authority in schools: a case study from Finland' in *Journal of Education for Teaching*, 26, 2:157-165

Tizard, B and Blatchford, P (1988) *Young Children at School in the Inner City*, London, Lawrence Erlbaum

Tizard, B; Blatchford, P; Burke, J; Farquahar, C and Plewis, I (1988) *Young Children at School in the Inner City,* London, Lawrence, Erlbaum

Troyna, B and Hatcher, R (1992) *Racism in Children's Lives – A study of Mainly White Primary Schools,* London, Routledge

Vygotsky, L (1991) Genesis of the Higher Mental Functions, in Light, P (ed) *Learning to Think*, London, Routledge

Vygotsky, L (1978) *Mind in Society, – The Development of Higher Psychological Processes*, London, Harvard University Press

Waksler, F.C (1996) *The Little Trials of Childhood and Children's Strategies for Dealing with Them*, London, Falmer

Walkerdine, V (1984) 'Developmental Psychology and the Child Centred Pedagogy: the Insertion of Piaget into Early Education, Henriques, J *et al* (eds) *Changing the Subject, Psychology, Social Regulation and Subjectivity,* London, Methuen

Watkinson, A. M (1996) Suffer the little children who come into schools' in Eppt, J.R and Watkinson, A.M. (eds) *Systemic Violence,* London, Falmer

Whyte, J (1995) *Changing Times: Challenges to Identity*, Aldershot: Avebury

Willmott, R (2001) The 'Mini-Renaissance' in Marxist Educational Sociology: a critique *British Journal of Sociology of Education*, Vol 22, No 2, 2001: 203-213

Willmott, R (1999) Structure, Agency and the Sociology of Education: rescuing analytical dualism in *British Journal of Sociology of Education*, Vol 20, No 1, 1999: 5-21

Willis, P (1977) *Learning to Labour: How Working Class Kids get Working Class Jobs*, Westmead, UK Saxon House

Willow, C (1990) *Hear! Hear! Promoting Children and Young People's Democratic participation in Local Government*, London, Local Government Information Unit

Woodhead, M (1990) Psychology and the Cultural Construction of Children's Needs. James, A and Prout, A *Constructing and Reconstructing Childhood*, Basingstoke, Falmer

Wyness, M (1999) 'Childhood, Agency and Education Reform, *Childhood* 6 (3): 353-68

Wyness, M (2000) *Contesting Childhood*, London, Falmer Press

Woods, P (1990) *The Happiest Days – How Pupils Cope with School,* Bristol, Falmer Press

Young, M (1970) *Knowledge and Control,* London, Collier MacMillan

Zeiher, H (2001) Children's Access to Space and Use of Time, Paper presented at the Cost A19 'Children's Welfare' meeting, Trondheim, Oct 26- 29

Zelizer, V (1985) *Pricing the Priceless Child – the Changing Social Value of Children*, New York, Basic Books

Index

ability differences 41, 56,
65, 66, 69, 96, 99,
103, 104, 107, 109
classification of
children by ability 56,
66, 104, 109
in curricular
preferences 41
in experience of
evaluation 96, 103,
107
in views of
pedagogical practice
56, 65, 69
views on cleverness
103-104
academic self image 100-
102
age differences 19, 17, 23,
85, 86, ,99, 102, 119
in views on
curriculum 39-42
in experience of
evaluation 94-95, 107
in views of
pedagogical practice
68-69, 74, 80-81, 88
teacher views on age
differences 24-25
agency 111, 126, 129
children as active
agents 4, 7, 50, 89,
108, 111, 120, 126-
130, 141-143

analytical pedagogy 114,133
attitudes to control 34
see also discipline
attitudes to school 139, 16,
128, 138, 134, 139
authoritative resources 122,
126

behaviour by gender 16, 73,
128
see also discipline
being good in school 105
see also socialisation
bullying/teasing 29, 30, 31,
72, 84, 106, 116, 139
see also child culture

child centred discourse 35,
117, 119-121, 126,
135, 141
child culture 2, 3, 31, 35,
45, 48-49, 92, 105-107
139, 142
and identity 35, 27
importance of 26, 29,
30, 33, 72
influence on curricular
experience 45, 48-49
reciprocity in 14
resistance to adult
norms 29, 31- 32, 35,
71, 82, 88, 108, 122,
146
school rules 80-83, 87

status and popularity
12, 27, 28, 30, 50, 88,
103
see also exercise of
power; school yard
child/adult relations 2-7, 4,
8, 37, 88, 91, 111,
115, 124, 128, 130,
145, *see also* social
theory
childhood as a structural
category 4, 124
socio-historical
analyses 3
sociology of childhood
3,5, 113, 133
structuring of
childhood 7, 50, 65,
88, 108-109, 111, 129,
135, 137, 140
time and space in 3,
8,34, 35, 37, 44, 53-
54, 65, 67, 73, 118,
120, 122, 125, 140
children as other 111-118,
120, 126, 131, 140
see also exercise of
power
citizenship 138, 143-148
and the curriculum
144
competition 48, 109, 127
see also child culture
control of time and space
67-71, 88